QUANTITATIVE STUDIES IN CRIMINOLOGY

Volume 8
SAGE RESEARCH PROGRESS SERIES IN CRIMINOLOGY

ABOUT THIS SERIES

The SAGE RESEARCH PROGRESS SERIES IN CRIMINOLOGY is intended for those professionals and students in the fields of criminology, criminal justice, and law who are interested in the nature of current research in their fields. Each volume in the series—four to six new titles will be published in each calendar year—focuses on a theme of current and enduring concern; and each volume contains a selection of previously unpublished essays . . . drawing upon presentations made at the previous year's Annual Meeting of the American Society of Criminology.

Now in its second year, the series continues with five new volumes, composed of papers presented at the 29th Annual Meeting of the American Society of Criminology held in Atlanta, Georgia on November 16-20, 1977. The volumes in this second year of publication include:

- *Violent Crime: Historical and Contemporary Issues*
  edited by James A. Inciardi and Anne E. Pottieger
- *Law and Sanctions: Theoretical Perspectives*
  edited by Marvin D. Krohn and Ronald L. Akers
- *The Evolution of Criminal Justice: A Guide for Practical Criminologists*
  edited by John P. Conrad
- *Quantitative Studies in Criminology*
  edited by Charles Wellford
- *Discretion and Control*
  edited by Margaret Evans

Previously published volumes include:

- *Theory in Criminology: Contemporary Views*
  edited by Robert F. Meier
- *Juvenile Delinquency: Little Brother Grows Up*
  edited by Theodore N. Ferdinand
- *Contemporary Corrections: Social Control and Conflict*
  edited by C. Ronald Huff
- *Criminal Justice Planning and Development*
  edited by Alvin W. Cohn

Comments and suggestions from our readers about this series are welcome.

SERIES EDITORS:

James A. Inciardi
University of Delaware

William E. Amos
U.S. Board of Parole

SAGE RESEARCH PROGRESS SERIES IN CRIMINOLOGY
VOLUME 8

QUANTITATIVE STUDIES IN CRIMINOLOGY

Edited by
Charles Wellford

Published in cooperation with the
AMERICAN SOCIETY OF CRIMINOLOGY

 SAGE Publications   Beverly Hills   London

Copyright © 1978 by Sage Publications, Inc.

For information address:

SAGE PUBLICATIONS, INC.
275 South Beverly Drive
Beverly Hills, California 90212

SAGE PUBLICATIONS LTD
28 Banner Street
London EC1Y 8QE

Printed in the United States of America

Library of Congress Cataloging in Publication Data
Main entry under title:

Quantitative studies in criminology.

(Sage research progress series in criminology; v. 8)
Papers presented at the 1977 meetings of the
American Society of Criminology.
Includes bibliographical references.

1. Crime and criminals—Methodology—Addresses, essays, lectures. 2. Criminal statistics—Addresses, essays, lectures.
I. Wellford, Charles F. II. American Society of Criminology.
III. Series.
HV6018.Q36   364'.01'8   78-19858
ISBN 0-8039-1130-0
ISBN 0-8039-1131-9 pbk.

CONTENTS

Charles Wellford
*Federal Justice Research
Program*

INTRODUCTION

In recent years criminologists have paid increasing attention to statistical and methodological issues. Beginning with the 1976 meetings of the American Society of Criminology special sessions were held to explore developments in statistics and methodologies that would be of particular interest to criminologists. The papers contained in this volume were selected from those delivered at the 1977 meetings of the American Society of Criminology, both in sessions specifically established to consider methodological and statistical issues as well as in sessions that were primarily substantive but raised important statistical and methodological issues.

For too long, criminologists have depended upon the development of methodology in related social science disciplines. For example, in recent years the econometrics literature has had significant impact on studies of deterrence and the increased use of regression-based techniques. The articles in this volume, however, address methodological issues within the particular confines of the problems that are faced by criminologists. The first section of the papers addresses the issue of measurement of crime. Although one can very helpfully draw from other social sciences to consider the problems of measurement, measuring crime represents certain problems that are not directly analogous to other areas of research. This point is most explicitly made in the chapter by George Bridges which considers the problem of self-report literature and applies statistical techniques to estimate the validity of such measurement techniques. Similarly the chapter by Petersilia considers the particular problems of validity associated with self-reported crime measurement. Galvin explores the concept of seriousness of crime to evaluate the process of legal socialization. Her chapter develops both substantive and methodological issues of relevance to the perception of crime.

One of the more difficult measurement problems in criminology in recent years concerns the concept of deterrence. Chapters by Logan and Cohen formulate new approaches to the methodology problems associated with deterrence and present data from recent studies to address these issues. Logan's paper emphasizes the limitation of aggregate data to test deterrence theory. Larry Cohen's chapter establishes a set of issues that can move deterrence research to the social psychological level where it can be more appropriately tested.

Another emergent theme in criminological methods is the emphasis on longitudinal studies. The works of Wolfgang et al. have demonstrated the importance of this approach to criminology and the papers by Shannon and Vigderhous demonstrate once again both the problems and value of this strategy for research. The latter paper, in addition, applies Box-Jenkins techniques to a frequently addressed criminological issue.

The final section of the volume contains a paper which applies quantitative techniques to the study of police performance. Richard Bennett's analysis of the role of education represents the application of regression techniques to important subjective issues in the consideration of the productivity and performance levels of police.

It is anticipated that each year the American Society of Criminology will select from its proceedings those papers that represent attempts to apply statistical methodology to important conceptual issues and thus stimulate the development of statistics and methodological applications to criminological problems. The works contained in the current volume demonstrate, at the same time, the increasing methodological sophistication of criminology and the need to continue our concerns with methodological issues raised by the topics and perspectives we research.

George Bridges
*United States
Department of Justice*

1

ERRORS IN THE MEASUREMENT OF CRIME
An Application of Joreskog's Method for the Analysis of General Covariance Structures

Measurement errors present troublesome problems in criminological research. If they are large and do not compensate for one another over subjects, then aggregate sample estimates of the volume or incidence of crime may be biased. Moreover, if they are unevenly distributed and more frequent and serious among some subjects than others, they may confound statistical relationships between measures of crime and explanatory variables such that these relationships are seriously attenuated.

Regardless of their source, these errors can be described as elements of measurement equations or models that depict the composition of observed scores. If we assume that measurements are linear (or can be transformed to

---

AUTHOR'S NOTE: This is a revision of a paper presented at the annual meeting of the American Society of Criminology in Atlanta, Georgia, 1977. The author gratefully acknowledges the support and advice of Professors Marvin Wolfgang, Philip Sagi, Robert Figlio, and Carlton Hornung on this project. The views presented herein do not reflect their views or the official position of the Department of Justice. The author accepts sole responsibility for the direction and content of this work.

linear form), a subject's score on a measure of crime can be formulated as,

$$x = \mu + \lambda x^* + \epsilon \qquad [1.1]$$

where x represents the observed incidence of crime (say the number of self-reported assaults), x^* represents the unobserved true value of that variable; λ reflects the effects of systematic measurement errors on reliability, and, ϵ a random error term. Subjects' observed scores then are equated to linear functions of unobserved true scores and random measurement errors.[1]

Efforts in modelling social phenomena address the effects of measurement error at length. Generally, this literature casts error in the context of deterministic models of variables from which these effects are derived. The simplest form of these models is diagrammed in Figure 1. Retaining the notation of equation 1.1, the unobserved variables, x_1^* and x_2^*, represent latent factors of which there are respectively p and q indicators or measured variables, each with a corresponding random error term $\epsilon_1, \epsilon_2, \epsilon_3, \ldots$ ϵ_{p+q}. In this model, the unobserved variables x_1^* and x_2^*, may be thought of as true scores, and $\lambda_{11}, \lambda_{12}, \lambda_{2p} \ldots , \lambda_{2p+q}$, as coefficients reflecting the reliability of the observed measures.

Much of the writing on these models restrict its treatment of error to the estimation method used in path analysis. Stimulated principally by the work of Costner (1969) and Blalock (1969), most of these studies deduce the presence of systematic errors from patterns among path coefficients (see for example, Sullivan, 1971; Jacobson and Lalu, 1974; Mayer and Younger, 1975). For the present purposes, however, it is sufficient to note that this approach presents difficult estimation problems (Hauser and Goldberger, 1971; Long, 1977). Moreover, means for testing the overall fit of the model to the observed correlations among variables until recently have not been available.

Recent papers and research by Joreskog (1959, 1970) develop and demonstrate an approach to estimating measurement error in systems of variables that overcomes the estimation problems of path analysis. Unlike path analysis,

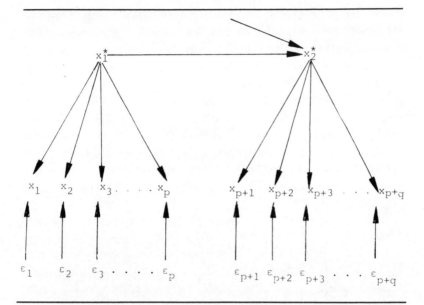

Figure 1: MODEL LINKING TWO UNOBSERVED VARIABLES EACH WITH MULTIPLE INDICATORS

Joreskog's method generalizes the principles of maximum-likelihood factor analysis to the treatment of general covariance structures. His approach relies on the principles of maximum-likelihood estimation and yields large sample estimates of model parameters that are asymptotically normal, efficient, and consistent. As Long points out, less technically these properties imply that the estimates are approximately normal, have minimum variance and tend to be unbiased in large samples. Also, we may test formal hypotheses about the goodness-to-fit of a particular model to the observed correlations among the measured variables with this technique. Several discussions and applications are found in the literature of sociology and psychology (Joreskog, 1969; Hauser and Goldberger; Werts et al., 1973, 1974; Costner and Schoenberg, 1973; Long; Bielby et al., 1977).

To explore and examine the extent and effects of error in different measures of crime, the remainder of this paper is devoted to an application of Joreskog's method. This application centers on the measurement errors in self-reported and official records of crime. The analysis begins with the simplest of multivariate models using multiple measures or indicators of hidden and official crimes. With this, we estimate the relationship between the unobserved or "true" levels of these variables as well as their relationships to the observed indicators. The model is then generalized to include the component of socio-economic status (SES) to examine the relationships between SES and subject's "true" hidden and official criminality. Throughout the analysis, critical attention is paid to the linkages among the indicators of hidden and official crimes to assess the types and magnitude of measurement errors that emerge in the solution.

MODEL

Joreskog's general model for the analysis of deterministic models differentiates between two types of statistical relationships: *structural* relationships between unobserved independent variables and unobserved dependent variables, and *measurement* relationships linking observed variables or indicators to these unobserved variables. The structural relationships are described in the standard form of a system of linear equations,

$$\beta \, \eta = \Gamma \, \xi + \zeta \qquad [1.2]$$

Wherein, η represents a set of m dependent variables, $\eta_1, \eta_2, \eta_3, \ldots, \eta_m$, and ξ represents a set of n independent, $\xi_1, \xi_2, \xi_3, \ldots, \xi_n$. The coefficients β and Γ in equation 1.2 represent (m x m) and (m x n) matrices of structural co-efficients relating the dependent and independent variables to each other. It should be obvious that in the instance of one dependent and one independent variable in a recursive or "one-way" system, β would be a scalar equal to 1 and Γ, analogous to an ordinary least squares regression weight. The factor ζ represents a set of errors in the equation that have E $(\zeta) = 0$ and are uncorrelated with ξ. Moreover, it is assumed that $E(\eta) = E(\xi) = 0$.

Because the variables described in η and ξ are considered unobserved, it is necessary to link these with the arrays of observed dependent and independent variables $\underset{\sim}{y}$ and $\underset{\sim}{x}$ where $\underset{\sim}{y} = y_1, y_2, y_3, \ldots, y_p$ and $\underset{\sim}{x} = x_1, x_2, x_3, \ldots, x_q$. Equation 1.1 can then be generalized to measurement equations for these multiple observed and unobserved variables such that

$$\underset{\sim}{y} = \mu + \Lambda_y \, \eta + \underset{\sim}{\epsilon} \qquad \text{[1.3]}$$
$$\underset{\sim}{x} = v + \Lambda_x \, \xi + \underset{\sim}{\delta} \qquad \text{[1.4]}$$

where $\underset{\sim}{\epsilon}$ and $\underset{\sim}{\delta}$ represent sets of random measurement errors in $\underset{\sim}{x}$ and $\underset{\sim}{y}$, and Λ_y and Λ_y are coefficient matrices linking the observed and unobserved variables. As noted earlier, the elements of Λ_x and Λ_y reflect the reliabilities of the observed variables. In addition to assumptions that the errors $\underset{\sim}{\epsilon}$ in $\underset{\sim}{\delta}$ and are uncorrelated with true scores such that

$$E\,(\underset{\sim}{\epsilon'\eta}) = E\,(\underset{\sim}{\delta'\eta}) = E\,(\underset{\sim}{\epsilon'\delta}) = E\,(\underset{\sim}{\epsilon'\xi}) = E\,(\underset{\sim}{\delta'\xi}) = 0$$

Joreskog lets ϕ (m x n) and Ψ (m x m) represent the variance-covariance matrices of ξ and ζ respectively and Θ_{ϵ}^2 (p x p) and Θ_{δ}^2 (q x q) the variance-covariance matrices of the terms in $\underset{\sim}{\epsilon}$ and $\underset{\sim}{\delta}$.

The overall model that is established equates an hypothesized covariance structure of observed variables Σ, to a system of structural and measurement equations described by the matrices $\Lambda_x, \Lambda_y, \beta, \Gamma, \phi, \Psi, \Theta_{\delta}^2$. The solution to the unknown elements of these matrices is derived principally from restricted or confirmatory factor analysis. A system of equations is specified by declaring each of the elements in these matrices as free for estimation fixed as constants, or constraints to equal one another. Assuming the ensuing model is identified—that is, that a unique solution can be reached—the estimation procedure minimizes the function F,

$$F = (1/2)\,\log|\Sigma| + \text{Tr}(S\Sigma^{-1}) - \text{Log}|S|\ \ (p+q),$$

where, S is the observed variance-covariance matrix of x and y. By minimizing F, this process minimizes, in effect, the difference between the observed variances and covariances in S and the covariance structure that is generated from the specified model. Hence, the estimation process fits the model of unobserved variables and elements of Λ_x, Λ_y, β, Γ, $\bar{\Phi}$, Ψ, $\Theta^2_{\bar{\epsilon}}$, and $\Theta^2_{\bar{\delta}}$ to the variances and covariances among the observed variables. This estimation can be performed with correlations equally well.

Hypothesis testing about this goodness of fit and thus, how well the overall model describes and explains relationships among the observed variables is performed with a likelihood ratio statistic that is approximately distributed as χ^2 with degrees of freedom, d, where

$$d = 1/2 \, (p + q) \, (p + q + 1) - s$$

and s is the total number independent elements of Λ_x, Λ_y, β, $\bar{\Phi}$, Ψ, $\Theta^2_{\bar{\epsilon}}$ and $\Theta^2_{\bar{\delta}}$ estimated in the model. Most simply, goodness-to-fit is measured in terms of the elements of the residual matrix. Hypotheses about the overall specification of the model are rejected when the magnitude of the residuals in Ψ falls above that expected at conventional levels of probability. Usually, a poor fit stems from the specification of an insufficient number of unobserved variables or an incorrect specification either of the correlations between observed and unobserved variables or the correlation of the measurement errors ϵ_1, ϵ_2 . . . ϵ_{p+q}.

Measures

In applying this method, our efforts center on measures of crime gathered in 1971 from a systematic sample (n = 567) of Philadelphia males born in 1945. These measures emerge from the work of Wolfgang, Figlio, and Sellin (1972) and reflect the official and hidden delinquency of the sample subjects. Personal interviews and police files were combined for the analysis. Seven measures of hidden and official criminality were selected to explore the "structural" and "measurement" relationships among these self-reported and official indices of crime. The measures of hidden crimes were chosen to reflect the volume of delinquencies unknown to officials. To ensure that both juvenile and adult offenses were represented in these measures, the following indicators were selected:

- *The Sum of All Hidden Offenses.* The total number of offenses reported in the personal interview as committed and unknown to the police.

- *The Sum of Hidden Index Offenses.* The total number of index offenses reported as committed and unknown to the police.

- *The Sum of All Hidden Offenses Committed Before Age 18.* The total number of offenses reported as committed before the age of 18 and unknown to the police.

- *The Ratio of Hidden Index Offenses Committed Before Age 18 and Total Hidden Offenses.* The simple ratio of hidden index offenses reported as committed before the age of 18 and unknown to the police, and the overall number of reported hidden offenses.

Whereas these measures reflect different elements of the volume of offenses escaping official visibility, three measures were constructed from the police files to reflect the volume and extent of contacts with law enforcement officials. These were:

- *The Sum of All Police Contacts.* The total number of police contacts resulting in the subject being taken into custody.

- *The Age at First Police Contact.* The subject's age at first contact with police in which he was taken into custody (age was calculated from the date of the contact).

- *The Length of Exposure to Police Contact.* The length of time (in years) between the subject's age at first contact with the police and age at last contact (up to the twenty-sixth year).

We view these seven measures only as indicators of the unobserved true levels of hidden and official crimes. Some may reflect these unobserved levels of crime more accurately than others and together they represent only a sample of all possible measures of crime. Consequently, the

Table 1: Correlations Between Indicators of Hidden and Official Delinquency

	Total Hidden Offenses	Total Hidden Offenses (Age LT 18)	Total Hidden Index	Ratio of Hidden Index to Total Offenses	Total Police Contacts	Age at First Contact	Length of Exposure to Police Contact
	1	2	3	4	5	6	7
1	1.000						
2	.763	1.000					
3	.510	.556	1.000				
4	-.053	.017	.527	1.000			
5	.155	.082	.061	.082	1.000		
6	-.096	.063	-.027	.063	-.328	1.000	
7	-.030	-.060	.059	-.060	.705	-.510	1.000

NOTE: The total sample consists of 567 subjects. Because of missing data, some of the correlations are based on a subsample of these subjects.

effects of measurement errors that are estimated herein are relative to our choice of indicators. And the measurement relationships we derive emerge from the correlations among these indicators.

It is important that the reader keep in mind that our constructs and the structural relationships we derive stem solely from these indicators and how we specify our analytical model. Clearly, other solutions might be obtained with other indicators of crime and by specifying the model differently.

With this caveat and the assumption that the relationship between hidden and official offenses can be described as recursive such that the incidence of hidden crimes influences the level of official crimes and not vice versa, the relationships among our observed indicators and unobserved variables are described as the model in Figure 1. The matrix of correlations among the indicators is presented in Table 1 and initially suggests that a weak positive correlation characterizes the link between official and hidden offenses—the strongest zero-order correlation among the

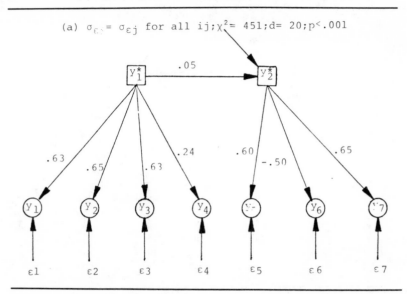

(a) $\sigma_{\epsilon i} = \sigma_{\epsilon j}$ for all ij; $\chi^2 = 451$; $d = 20$; $p < .001$

Figure 2: MEASUREMENT MODELS OF SELF-REPORTED AND OFFICIAL CRIMES

indicators is that between the volume of hidden offenses and the volume of police contacts (r = .155).

Findings

The model presented in Figure 2 describes a network of relationships between our indicators and unobserved variables. To explore the role of measurement errors in this model, we initially estimate the structural and measurement coefficients under an hypothetical *absence* of correlated measurement errors, unequal error variances, and measurement bias. This simulates what would be expected under the conventional assumptions of an ordinary least squares solution to these coefficients. Figure 3a presents this solution and indicates that a weak positive structural relationship exists between the volume of hidden and official crime ($\gamma = .05$). Moreover, few of the measurement coefficients, λ_{ij}, are strong. Under the imposed assumptions then no single indicator very accurately reflects either unobserved variable. Indeed, the measurement coefficients do not exceed .65.

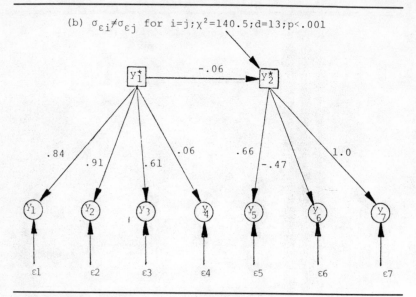

(b) $\sigma_{\varepsilon i} \neq \sigma_{\varepsilon j}$ for $i=j; \chi^2=140.5; d=13; p<.001$

Figure 2 (Continued)

The large chi-square statistic indicates a sizable discrepancy between the observed correlational structure (the correlation matrix of the indicators) and the structure reproduced with the specified model. This suggests there is some misspecification of the structural and measurement relationships—that is, some of the imposed assumptions are not supported in the data. Figures 2b and 2c present solutions to the model as these assumptions about the types and magnitude of measurement errors are relaxed. The overall fit of the models to the observed correlations generally improves as more elements or parameters in the model are estimated and fewer constraints are imposed on the variances and correlations among error terms $\varepsilon_1, \varepsilon_2, \ldots \varepsilon_7$.

Figure 2b presents the estimated solution under an hypothesis of unequal or heteroscedastic error variances. By introducing heteroscedasticity, most of the measurement coefficients increase in their absolute value. A slight change in the structural coefficient—γ_{12}—from positive to negative is also apparent. Although the chi-square statistic in this instance falls beyond that expected at conventional

(c) $\sigma_{\varepsilon_{ij}} \neq \sigma_{\varepsilon_j}$ for all ij; $\chi^2=23.1$; d=10; p=.01

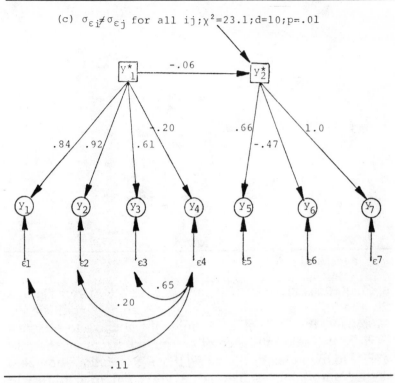

Figure 2 (Continued)

levels of probability, its pronounced difference in magnitude from that of 3a suggests that much greater variation in the observed variables is explained. Isolating differences in the error variances of our indicators then further clarifies the linkages between our observed and unobserved variables. Even though a large amount of variation remains unexplained (p > .001), the volume of hidden offenses committed before the age of 18 appears as the strongest indicator of the volume of hidden offenses and exposure to police contact—the length of subject's contact history—as the strongest indicator of the volume of official contacts.

To gain a clearer description of the model underlying our data, the correlations of errors between indicators were estimated for indicators in which the residuals from the solution in 2b were larger. The results of this estimation are

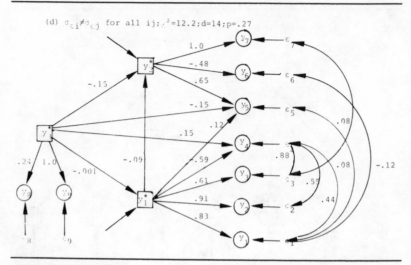

Figure 2 (Continued)

presented in Figure 2c.[2] Little change is evident from Figures 2b and 2c in the structural and measurement coefficients. Moreover, the shift of λ_{14} from slight positive to negative mirrors the sole influence of correlated errors on the reliability of the indicators. Finding these correlations non-zero is not surprising—subjects may respond to batteries of items or questions consistently, albeit inaccurately. In this instance, the correlations suggest errors in reporting the volume of serious hidden offenses and are linked to errant reporting on the relative seriousness and volume of all hidden offenses. The pronounced improvement in the goodness-to-fit of this model suggests that the inclusion of correlated errors aids in explaining the observed correlations among our indicators.

A third source of measurement error in deterministic models is Costner's "differential bias" and consists of error variation attributed to an unobserved variable or construct other than that which the indicator is thought to measure. For example, an indicator of official crimes—the number of police contacts—may be influenced by the true volume of hidden offenses as well as the true or unobserved number of offenses acted upon by police. The police may

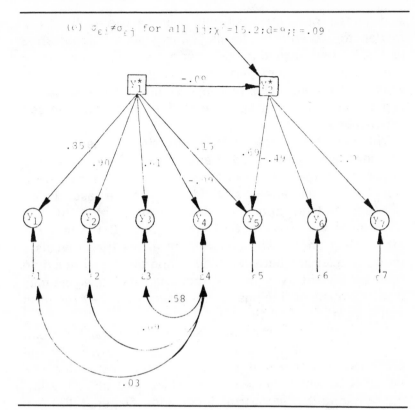

Figure 2 (Continued)

record contacts with those committing a higher volume of offenses more frequently than they record the contacts of those committing fewer offenses. Insofar as this may systematically distort police records, it may be considered a source of systematic measurement bias.

To explore this type of error in our model, the measurement coefficients λ_{21}, λ_{23}, and λ_{15} were estimated. The residuals remaining from the solution in 3c suggested this specification. The estimation is presented in Figure 3d. Although few changes in the structural and measurement coefficients result from this respecification, we observe that differential bias has its greatest impact on the number of recorded police contacts. Moreover, adding this path and those leading to our measures of the volume of all hidden and hidden index offenses improves the overall fit of the model to acceptable levels of statistical significance ($p > .05$). Yet because these latter paths approximate zero, a final estimation was performed fixing λ_{21} and λ_{23} at zero. Presented in Figure 3e, this final solution demonstrates a slightly better fit of the hypothesized model to the observed correlations.

This solution reveals at least one striking result on the relationship between hidden and official crimes, and more generally on the measurement of crime. Whereas conventional bivariate analysis yields a positive association between hidden and official offenses ($r = .155$), the association we derive is weak and negative. Controlling the attenuating effects of measurement errors then reveals a much weaker link between hidden and official crimes than otherwise is observed. Indeed, this suggests that errors may distort statistical findings to the extent that they result in seriously misleading findings.

Our treatment of measurement error thus far has been limited to a special problem in factor analysis. In the presence of correlated errors, we have estimated the linkages between indicators of hidden and official delinquency and their latent true dimensions. To generalize this treatment to a more complex system of variables, a third structural variable of SES is introduced into the model. By employing two indicators of SES—y_8 (the North-Hart rating of the father's occupational prestige) and y_9 (median family income for the census tract resided in at age 18)—a recursive system of simultaneous linear equations among our structural variables, can be established such that,

$$y_1^* = \beta_{13} Y_3^* \qquad\qquad + \zeta_1 \qquad\qquad [1.5]$$

$$y_2^* = \beta_{21} y_1^* + \beta_{23} \ y_3^* + + \zeta_2 \qquad\qquad [1.6]$$

Herein, SES (y_3^*) is viewed as an unobserved independent variable and hidden and official delinquency as unobserved dependent variables.

Estimation under this new model is presented in Figure 3a. This reveals negative structural relationships between

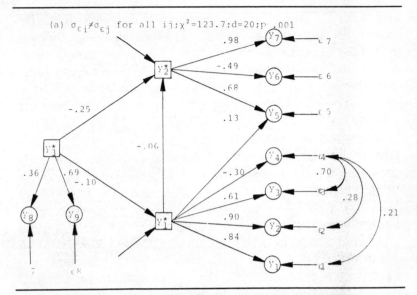

Figure 3: STRUCTURAL EQUATION MODELS OF SELF-REPORTED CRIMES, AND SES WITH MEASUREMENT ERRORS

SES and hidden and official crimes. Consistent in part with the findings of other research, this negative relationship is stronger for official offenses than hidden offenses. Moreover, all but one of the measurement coefficients from Figure 2e is unchanged; λ_{14} shifts from -.09 to -.30, reflecting the effect of SES on subjects' unobserved number of hidden offenses and how these offenses are recorded. This effect is also evident in the correlations among the errors—these correlations dramatically increase in magnitude. The high test statistic in this model (p > .001) suggests, however, that a better fit with the observed data might be obtained by re-specifying some of its structural and measurement paths. The estimations under these respecifications are presented in Figures 3b-3d.

To examine whether differential measurement bias linking SES and indicators of official crimes is operant—that is, whether the biases in our indicators of official crimes are linked to subject's SES—two paths between SES and our measures of official offenses are estimated. Presented in Figure 3b, the results of this estimation are

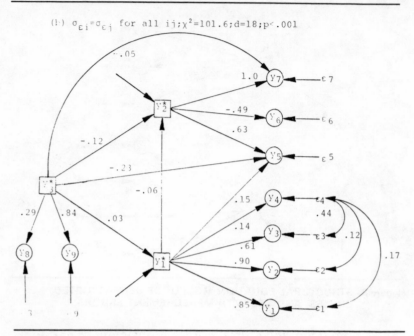

Figure 3 (Continued)

provoking. First, the structural coefficient linking SES and official delinquency is halved—only a slight inverse relationship is demonstrated between the "true" volume of official offenses and SES. Second, an inverse relationship between SES and the recorded number of police contacts is discovered suggesting that the inverse relationship evident between "true" official crimes and SES in Figure 3a may have been artifactual and stemmed, in part, from this measurement bias. Furthermore, the solution suggests that there is a weaker relationship between all offenses acted upon by the police and SES than for those offenses which are recorded. Although we are tempted to conclude from this finding that police records incorrectly reflect the true relationship between official delinquency and SES, there is a disappointingly weak structural fit between the model and the observed variances and covariances ($p > .001$).

It is also possible that differential bias operates on our measures of hidden delinquency. Estimates of the para-

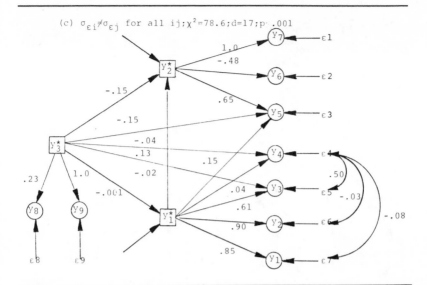

(c) $\sigma_{\varepsilon i} \neq \sigma_{\varepsilon j}$ for all ij; $\chi^2 = 78.6$; d=17; p .001

Figure 3 (Continued)

meters linking SES and two of our interview measures were made with the coefficient λ_{32} fixed at zero (its high standard error suggested that it is probably zero). This yielded the solution presented in Figure 3c. As above, we find a better but nonetheless weak fit between the model and the observed correlations. The chi-square statistic, albeit reduced, remains very large. The added measurement coefficients λ_{34} and λ_{34} suggest that some differential bias is presented in the interview measures. Moreover, the coefficient λ_{34} has a low standard error suggesting it is statistically significant and should be retained in the model.

Because measurement errors among constructs may also be correlated, a final effort was made to identify the role of non-random errors in the model and reach, if possible, a better fit with the observed correlational structure. Moreover, the absence of residual correlations among our indicators of official crimes and the pronounced evidence of residual correlations between the indicators of hidden and official crimes suggested that these cross-construct correlations among errors non-zero. To explore their patterns, the correlations of errors between indicators

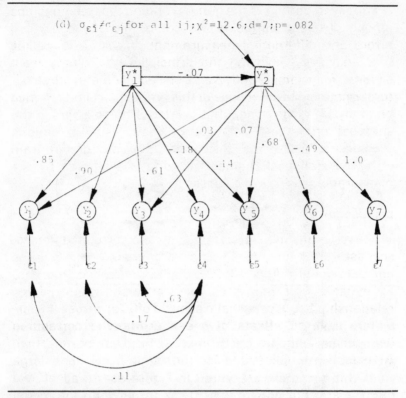

Figure 3 (Continued)

having the highest residual correlations are estimated and are presented in Figure 3d.[3]

This solution to our system of equations is encouraging. Apart from the dramatic improvement in the models' fit to the observed correlational structure, we find that the addition of cross-construct correlated errors amplifies the correlation of errors between the interview measures as well as the measurement coefficient linking y_4 to "true" hidden delinquency (λ_{14} = .-59). Because our construct of hidden offenses is related principally in offenses committed by juveniles, its strong inverse relationship with the ratio of hidden index to all hidden offenses also suggests that the unobserved or "true" level of hidden offenses may disproportionately consist of non-index offenses.

Equally important is the general finding that relationships among observed variables are confounded by correlated errors and differential measurement biases. This implies that analyses employing the principles of ordinary least squares for example may yield biased estimates of structural relationships. Because of this problem, a blind reliance on analytical approaches that overlooks these errors in the study of crime and delinquency may result in serious problems of inference. Inferences that are drawn from observed statistical relationships may be vitiated by the measurement errors we observe.

DISCUSSION

These results indicate that biases and correlated heteroscedastic errors may seriously distort our measures of crime and delinquency. Adding paths of differential bias from SES to indicators of police contact reveals an unexpected relationship between social class and official crimes. In partialling out the effects of these errors, the correlation between SES and official offenses diminishes significantly. At least two implications for the study of crime emerge from this finding. First, measures of hidden and official crimes are subject to troublesome systematic errors. Because of this, relationships between measures of crime and explanatory variables such as SES may be confounded. In the absence of statistical controls, these systematic errors may vitiate inferences that are drawn about the distribution of crimes in the general population.

A second implication, moreover, is that the effects of these errors may be estimated in multivariate measurement models. Identifying these effects in a system of structural and measurement equations, we identify the influence of error on relationships among our observed and unobserved variables. This results in a network of relationships deduced from the correlations among observed indicators that is, by hypothesis, free of measurement error. Even though we are limited to studying the effects of an unmeasured and hypothetical error structure, Joreskog's method permits a rigorous treatment of the measurement error problem. Moreover, it provides an important avenue for substantive inquiry that accounts for the errors in the fallible measures we commonly employ.

NOTES

1. Under the assumption that x and x* respectively represent observed and true scores on a single variable, λ^2 is the reliability coefficient of the observed score x. This coefficient reflects the level of systematic non-random error in the observed score (see Guilford, 1954: ch. 4; Lord and Novick, 1969: ch. 12). This is readily demonstrated.

If x_1 and x_2 are parallel measures of x* then

$$\lambda_{x1} = \lambda_{x2} = \lambda_x \text{ and,}$$

$$E(r_{x1x2}) = \frac{E\ (\lambda_x x^* + \epsilon_1)\ (\lambda_x x^* + \epsilon_2)}{\sigma_x^2}$$

$$= \frac{\lambda_x^2\ \sigma_x^2}{\sigma_x^2} + \frac{E(\lambda_x x^* \epsilon_1)}{\sigma_x^2} + \frac{E(\lambda_x x^* \epsilon_2)}{\sigma_x^2} + \frac{E(\epsilon_1,\ \epsilon_2)}{\sigma_x^2}$$

$$= \lambda_x^2 \text{ by the assumption that}$$

$$E(x,\epsilon) = E(x^*,\epsilon) = E(\epsilon,\epsilon) = 0$$

2. Two difficulties were encountered in estimating the model under this hypothesis. Freeing correlations among all errors led to the under-identified model. Consequently, the correlations were selected for estimation from the patterns of residual first-derivatives of the information matrix from the solution in Figure 3b. Those correlations among indicators with the highest residuals and first derivatives were specified as free; those that were approximately zero were fixed at zero.

3. We should stress that there is no evidence in the residual matrix or in the first derivatives of the information matrix that the measures of official delinquency had correlated errors. Because of this, cross-construct correlated errors are estimated for those solutions with high residuals, first derivatives, or both.

REFERENCES

BIELBY, W. T., R. M. HAUSER, and D. L. FEATHERMAN (1977) "Response errors of black and non-black males in models of intergenerational transmission of socio-economic status." Amer. J. of Sociology 82, 6: 1242-1287.

BLALOCK, H. M., Jr. (1969) "Multiple indicators and the causal approach to measurement error." Amer. J. of Sociology 75: 264-272.

COSTNER, A. L. (1969) "Theory, deduction, and rules of correspondence." Amer. J. of Sociology 75: 245-263.

——— and R. SCHOENBERG (1972) "Diagnosing indicator ills in multiple indicator models," pp. 168-200 in A. S. Goldberger and O. D. Duncan (eds.) Structural Equation Models in the Social Sciences. New York: Seminar Press.

GUILFORD, G. P. (1954) Psychometric Methods. New York: McGraw-Hill.

HAUSER, R. M. and A. S. GOLDBERGER (1971) "The treatment of unobservable variables in path analysis," pp. 81-117 in H. L. Costner (ed.) Sociological Methodology, 1971. San Francisco: Jossey-Bass.

HIRSCHI, T. (1969) Causes of Delinquency. Berkeley: Univ. of California Press.

JACOBSON, A. L. and N. M. LALU (1974) "An empirical and algebraic analysis of alternative techniques for measuring unobserved variables," pp. 215-242 in H. M. Blalock, Jr. (ed.) Measurement of the Social Sciences. Chicago: Aldine.

JORESKOG, K. G. (1970) "A general method for the analysis of covariance structure." Biometrika 57: 239-251.

——— (1969) "A general approach to confirmatory maximum likelihood factor analysis." Psychometrika 34: 183-202.

——— and D. SORBOM (1976) "LISREL III-estimation of linear structural equation systems by maximum likelihood methods." Chicago: National Educational Resources.

LONG, J. S. (1976) "Estimation and hypothesis testing in linear models containing measurement error." Soc. Methods and Research 5, 2: 157-206.

LORD, F. and M. NOVICK (1969) Statistical Theories of Mental Test Scores. Reading, MA: Addison-Wesley.

MAYER, L. S. and M. S. YOUNGER (1975) "Multiple indicators and the relationship between abstract variables," pp. 191-211 in D. R. Heise (ed.) Sociological Methodology. San Francisco: Jossey Bass.

SULLIVAN, J. L. (1971) "Multiple indicators and complex causal models," in H. M. Blalock, Jr. (ed.) Causal Models in the Social Sciences. Chicago: Aldine.

WERTS, C. E., R. L. LINN, and K. G. JORESKOG (1974) "Quantifying unmeasured variables," pp. 270-297 in H. M. Blalock, Jr. (ed.) Measurement in the Social Sciences. Chicago: Aldine.

——— (1971) "Estimating the parameters of path models involving unmeasured variables," in H. Blalock (ed.) Causal Models in the Social Sciences. Chicago: Aldine.

WOLFGANG, M. E., R. M. FIGLIO, and J. SELLIN (1972) Thorsten Delinquency in a Birth Cohort. Chicago: Univ. of Chicago Press.

2

Joan Petersilia
Rand Corporation

THE VALIDITY OF CRIMINALITY DATA DERIVED FROM PERSONAL INTERVIEWS

The extent of crime committed by persons of various characteristics (e.g., age, race, socioeconomic status) has been a core criminological issue. Much of the research in the field has focused on how to obtain valid estimates of crime commission rates. It is well known that an individual's official criminal record ("rap sheets") provides inaccurate estimates of the extent to which he commits crime. The reason is simple—since relatively few criminal acts lead to an arrest, rap sheets systematically underestimate an individual's level of crime. Dissatisfaction with official records has stimulated the use of alternative methods of measuring individual criminal behavior, such as questionnaires, telephone surveys, and personal interviews.

The personal interview appears to be the most promising method for obtaining complex criminality information. By interviewing, one may reduce errors due to poor motivation, reading inability, and lack of comprehension. Interviews can also draw out the details of an offense in order to establish whether a crime was committed, question

AUTHOR'S NOTE: Prepared under Grant Number 77-NI-99-0053 from the National Institute of Law Enforcement and Criminal Justice, Law Enforcement Administration, U. S. Department of Justice. Points of view or opinions stated in this document are those of the author and do not necessarily represent the official position or policies of the U. S. Department of Justice. This paper was prepared for a panel on "Validation of Self-Report Measures," 1977 American Society of Criminology.

possible exaggerations, and clear up misunderstandings. As was recently pointed out:

> It is clear that the interview method is preferable for certain purposes, especially when the inquiry is concerned to classify crime in terms of seriousness and frequency. A seriousness scale must be based on an assessment of the actual circumstances of the offense, and the frequency counts, relying on memory as they do, can be checked more thoroughly through the searching promptings of an interview. If questions are asked about a restricted number of items, the interviewer can aid the respondent considerably in problems of recall. It is suggested that in the self-completion situation either he will simply guess an approximate number or plump for a simple category such as "occasionally" or "frequently". (Hood and Sparks, 1971)

Those who object to the interview method frequently do so on the grounds that it precludes the respondent's anonymity. However, the desirability of anonymity in criminological research is not clearly established by the empirical evidence. Hyman has cautioned that the "literal fact of anonymity provides no necessary psychological anonymity" (Ball, 1967), and some criminological researchers have concluded that anonymity is unnecessary, overemphasized, or of little consequence.

The interview method is not without problems. Although it is generally assumed that valid—that is, "truthful"— responses can be obtained if proper interview procedures are followed, this assumption has received little empirical testing. In instances where validity checks have been made, it has been shown that interview responses contain elements of inaccuracy, even on simple questions such as age or possession of a telephone. On more complex questions, or those that are socially sensitive, validity is expected to diminish further. The findings of the few existing validity studies of interview data suggest:

> When people are being interviewed directly concerning behavior about which there is strong expectation of social approval or disapproval, and in which there is considerable ego-involvement, they tend to err in the direction of idealizing their behavior. (Maccoby and Maccoby, 1972)

Given this finding, the validity of criminality data obtained via interview is particularly vulnerable to challenge because criminal behavior is not only disapproved but subject to legal sanctions. Unfortunately, there has been little research on the issue; and that which has been done has usually ignored differences by crime types or recall periods. Further, the vast majority of studies using the interview method have concentrated exclusively on juvenile populations.[1] Much more validity research will be required to ascertain whether the personal interview is an appropriate technique for measuring the extent of a person's involvement in crime and delinquency.

The research in this chapter proceeds as follows. First, findings are presented on the extent of the offender's criminal behavior, relative to the amount for which he was officially arrested and convicted. The information was collected during personal interviews. Second, the validity of the interview data is assessed by comparing the self-reported information on arrests and convictions with rap sheet data. The validity discussion concerns the overall validity of the responses, as well as the validity associated with different crime types, "recall periods," and interviewer gender.

The Research

The data presented in this chapter derives from a larger research project entitled "Criminal Careers of Habitual Felons." The study focuses on the criminal careers of 49 inmates of a medium-security prison in California. All were serving time for armed robbery and all had served at least one prior prison term. We believed that the fact of current incarceration for armed robbery was a valid indicator of dangerous criminal conduct and that the record of at least one prior prison term was a valid indicator of persistent serious criminal activity.

The study was undertaken to systematically examine the changes which occur as an offender develops a career in crime.[2] Of particular interest were changes associated with family relationships, employment, crime motivation, alcohol and drug use, criminal sophistication, and the extent of crime commission, arrest, and conviction. This chapter restricts its discussion to the crime commission, arrest, and conviction results.

To obtain a population of felons meeting the foregoing criteria, we requested assistance from the California Department of Corrections (CDC), which secured the cooperation of the warden of California Men's Colony (CMC) at San Luis Obispo, California. The research division provided a random list of nearly 60 appropriate felons.

Each prospective interviewee was sent a notice asking that he appear at the interviewing station at a specified time. The inmate was met individually by a Rand interviewer, the purposes and nature of the interview were explained, and his participation requested. As it turned out, one of the original candidates had already been transferred to another institution, four did not appear because of visitor's day commitments, and three declined for other reasons. The remainder were interviewed. One interviewee's responses were discarded because he appeared to be under the influence of narcotics during the interview. In all, 49 interviews were used in the analysis.

The interview instrument. The interview instrument was a highly structured questionnaire consisting of both open- and closed-ended questions. To allow the systematic tracing of changes during a career, it was administered in sections corresponding to three contiguous career periods: (1) *juvenile,* from the first reported juvenile offense through the first juvenile incarceration, or until age 18 if no juvenile incarceration; (2) *young adult,* from release after the first juvenile incarceration through the first adult incarceration; and (3) *adult,* from release after the first adult incarceration to the time of the interview in the current confinement. Approximately two hundred questions were repeated in each career section. By comparing the behavior that occurred in the three periods, we are able to produce data that would illuminate changes that occur as offenders continue to pursue a life in crime.

For each of the three specified time periods, the offender was asked to recall the number of times he committed each of nine representative types of offenses during each of the three contiguous periods in his criminal career.

The crime types considered were auto theft, grand larceny, aggravated assault, burglary, robbery, rape, and drug sale.[3] For these offenses he was also asked to recall the number of times he was arrested and convicted. These items were assembled into a "crime matrix" pertaining to the events of each career period (see Fig. 1 for the form of the crime matrix).

The validity of the information. To verify some of the interview information, we obtained the state and federal criminal justice records for each of the interviewees. Before the interviews, we recorded the date on which each period of incarceration exceeding 60 days began. One purpose was to identify the dates of the three study-defined career periods for each interviewee. At the opening of an interview, we asked the respondent to confirm each period of incarceration we had recorded from his rap sheet and to supply information on how long each of the incarcerations lasted. This review helped to refresh the respondent's memory about the order of events in his past, and it also diminished the "halo effect" in his response, since it made him aware that we had knowledge of some of the entries on his official record.

The crime matrix used in the interview covered the respondent's *offenses, arrests,* and *convictions* (*not* incarcerations).

After the interviews, as a validity check, we returned to the respondents' rap sheets and compared the recorded information on dates of arrest, the charges, and whether a conviction resulted, with the corresponding information from the respondent. Each self-reported arrest or conviction item was considered "validated" only if the official record showed an arrest or conviction for the same crime type during the specific dates we had identified as the beginning and end of each crime period.

Conduct of the interviews. The interviews were conducted in private rooms, with only the inmate and the interviewer present; no correctional officer was within hearing distance. To encourage candor and avoid administrative complications, the interviews were not tape-recorded. Six Rand staff members, all experienced in interviewing offenders, conducted the interviews, which ran about two hours each.

To enhance the validity of the interviewees' responses, we followed certain procedures recommended in the literature.

- No one associated with the correctional institution was permitted to assist in conducting the interviews.

- The interviewer explained to the respondent that the interview would be complex in asking him to remember details of his life in three periods. The respondent was encouraged to ask for clarification if he did not understand a question and not to answer unless it was clear to him.

- The respondent was assured that he could decline to answer any question, and he was encouraged to do so if he could not answer honestly.

- The interviewer began by asking nonthreatening questions (e.g., about family, education, and employment) and reserved the questions about criminality for later in the interview.

- To help respondent accurately recall the events of a certain career period, the interviewer described what the respondent was doing at the beginning and end of the period (e.g., "You had just graduated from Grant High School and were living with your sister on Alvarado Street."). We obtained this "anchoring" information from official presentence reports.

- In asking questions requiring a categorical answer (always, sometimes, never), the interviewer gave the respondent a printed card showing the choices, to avoid "response patterning."

- In several of the open-ended questions, the respondent was allowed to digress, in order to build rapport with the interviewer and to reduce fatigue. Most of this information was not recorded.

THE RESEARCH FINDINGS

The remainder of this chapter presents the research results. The first section reports the extent of criminal behavior the sample reported committing and the prob-

Figure 1: CRIME MATRIX (REPEATED FOR EACH CAREER PERIOD)

Question: Now I am going to read you a list of criminal offenses. Please tell me whether you did any of these during your juvenile period; your young adult period; your adult period?

NOTE: Juvenile period: from the first self-reported offense through the first juvenile incarceration, or, if no juvenile incarceration, until age 18. Young adult period: from release after the first juvenile incarceration through the first adult incarceration. Adult period: from release after the first adult incarceration to the time of the Rand interview in the current incarceration.

abilities of arrest and conviction. The second section assesses the validity of the self-reported information. The chapter concludes with a recapitulation and interpretation of the research findings.

The Extent of Self-Reported
Crimes, Arrests, and Convictions

The most interesting and policy-relevant characteristic of criminal activity is its variation in intensity and seriousness over time. Habitual offenders are commonly thought to account for disproportionately large amounts of crime. The issue is how much crime and what types?

As previously mentioned, we asked the respondents to estimate, for each career period and for each of nine types of crime, how many times they committed the crime, how many times they were arrested, and how many times convicted. The total number and relative frequency of each offense type are shown by career period in Table 1.

Extent and patterns of criminality. For the nine offense types about which they were asked, the 49 respondents reported committing a total of 10,505 offenses—an average of 214 per offender. Since these crimes were committed over an average career span of 18 to 21 years, with the street time of these offenders averaging only about 10 years, we note that the average crime commission rate for the sample of interviewees was 20 offenses per year.[4]

The offense rate varied considerably by crime class. The average number of violent crimes (rape, assault, robbery, purse snatching) committed per year of street time was 1.8, safety crimes (violent crimes plus burglary), 5.9, and nondrug crimes (safety crimes plus auto theft, grand theft, and forgery), 11.0.

The offense rate was related to maturation. The number of self-reported offenses committed per month of street time noticeably declined as the sample grew older. Specifically, the juvenile period average of 3.2 serious crimes per month of street time decreased to 1.5 in the young adult period and to 0.6 in the adult period. Declining offense rates were also shown in each crime class except violent crimes, which were dominated by robbery. The latter anomaly probably is due to the sample selection criterion

Table 1: Self-Reported Crime Commission, Arrest, and Conviction Totals for the 49 Interviewees

Offense Type	Juvenile Period			Young Adult Period			Adult Period			Full Career		
	Number Committed	Arrest Rate[a] (%)	Conviction Rate[b] (%)	Number Committed	Arrest Rate[a] (%)	Conviction Rate[b] (%)	Number Committed	Arrest Rate[a] (%)	Conviction Rate[b] (%)	Number Committed	Arrest Rate[a] (%)	Conviction Rate[b] (%)
Auto theft	848	3	2	558	2	1	36	5	3	1,492	3	2
Purse snatch	20	15	5	5	20c	0c	0	0	0	25	16	4
Theft over $50	433	1	1	417	0c	0c	143	1	0	993	1	1
Burglary	1,458	2	2	791	2	2	82	5	2	2,331	2	2
Robbery	11	36	27	405	5	5	439	11	10	855	8	8
Aggravated assault	103	16	13	56	9	4	29	0	0	188	12	8
Forgery/NSF	363	2	2	489	4c	3c	143	3	3c	995	3c	2c
Drug sales	1,262	0	0	1,754	0c	0c	604	1	0c	3,620	0	0c
Rape	3	100	100	2	100	100	1	100	100	6	100	100
Total	4,551	2.2	1.6	4,477	1.9	1.4	1,477	4.3	3.8	10,505	2.4	1.8
Total (excluding rape and drug sales)	3,286	3.0	2.2	2,721	2.9	2.1	872	6.7	6.1	6,879	3.4	2.6

a. Arrest rate is the percentage of offense commissions that result in arrest.
b. Conviction rate is the percentage of offense commissions that result in conviction.
c. Indicates percentage less than 0.5.

that the current incarceration was for a robbery conviction.

Excluding drug sales, which were the most common crime but were committed by a small minority, the most common crime type for the group as a whole was burglary, especially during the first two periods. Both auto theft and burglary show the relative decline expected as offenders progress from juvenile property crime to adult predatory crime.

These offenders did not specialize in a single type of crime for any length of time. About 70% switched their principal offense type between successive career periods. The median number of crime types committed in any one period was three.

Arrest rate and conviction rate. Two revealing measures of the performance of the criminal justice system in dealing with an individual offender are the number of crimes that he commits relative to the frequency of his arrests and convictions, or from the offender's point of view, they are measures of his crime proficiency. Table 1 contains arrest rates and conviction rates by offense type and by period of the criminal career period, calculated from the self-reported information.

The results for the nine crime types combined, calculated for the full criminal career, show that only 2.4% of the self-reported commissions resulted in an arrest, 1.8% in conviction. If we exclude rape and drug sales from the calculation (which tend to represent the extremes), the arrest rate for the full career is 3.4, and the conviction rate is 2.6.

These rates differ markedly if we examine the various crime types separately. For instance, for the full career, the crimes of person (aggravated assault, purse snatch, robbery, and rape) have the highest arrest rate—from 8.5% to 16% for the first three, and 100% for rape.

It is noteworthy that for the crime of robbery the rate of arrest declined through the criminal career from 36% in the juvenile period to 8% in the adult period, and for the rate of conviction, from 27% to 8%. This change probably reflected greater proficiency on the part of the offender in terms of crime preparation and arrest avoidance at later stages of his career. The 100% arrest rate and conviction rate for rape most likely implies that offenders reported only rapes that were officially detected.

The Validity of the Arrest and Conviction Information

Although there is no practical means to validate the rates the offenders reported *committing* crimes, their official records provide a means to validate the responses they gave regarding how many times they had been arrested and convicted for each of the nine crime types. This validation procedure has already been discussed. Below we present the results of comparing the self-reported information on arrests and convictions with the same information on official records.

The overall validity of the responses. The 47 offenders for whom rap sheets could be obtained reported a total of 239 arrests over their entire careers for the specified offense types. By comparison, their rap sheets contained 364 arrests for these offense types. Therefore, the offenders reported 63% of the arrests contained on their official records.

The offenders reported a total of 185 convictions for the nine offense types. By comparison, their rap sheets showed a total of 245 convictions from arrests for these offense types, with 206 resulting in incarceration of more than 60 days. Comparing these data, we found that the number of self-reported convictions was 74% of the official number and 88% of the number ending in significant incarceration (and therefore more memorable). This favorable comparison is somewhat weakened when we examine individual career periods.

Juvenile convictions were considerably underreported on rap sheets since juvenile arrests are typically not recorded there (except for those that end in reformatory incarcerations). This was confirmed by our interviewees, who reported 69 convictions for the specified offense types during the first career period, while their rap sheets contained only 23.

In order to correct for this systematic bias, we deleted both the self-reported and rap sheet data pertaining to the juvenile period from the analysis concerning crime types.

Validity by crime type, interview period, and gender of interviewer. In Table 2, the total number of arrests and convictions the offender reported for the two adult career periods are compared to those that appear in his official records. This table facilitates the examination of the overall validity of this information, the relation between type of crime and validity, and the effect of the different interview periods.

We compared the total number of arrests and convictions the offender reported for the two adult career periods with those appearing in his official records. For those two periods, the offenders were found to have reported roughly half of their official arrests and convictions.

By crime type. The use of self-reported techniques raises the issue of whether some types of deviant behavior are likely to be underreported or overreported during personal interviews. Previous research has suggested that reporting bias depends on the gravity of the offense. Gold (1966) found overreporting of trivial offenses, and Farrington (1973) ascertained that there was underreporting of serious offenses. This is consistent with earlier work by Clark and Tifft (1966), which showed that offenses thought to be "never permissible were underreported." The explanation is that if the respondent wants to present himself in the best light, he will underreport the more stigmatizing offenses.

However, some recent research has contradicted this notion. Respondents have been found to underreport *less* stigmatizing offenses to a greater degree than more stigmatizing ones. As a possible explanation, one author suggested

> this result may occur because people are not willing to lie about unambiguous facts. However, behaviors which are ambiguous as to their definition of offenses, and which are engaged in frequently so that their number is difficult to remember, may well be subject to self-enhancing definitions in threatening situations. The occasions in which a person takes money from someone by force are probably remembered fairly clearly. To fail to report these offenses would require a knowing outright lie on the part of the respondents. (Teilman, 1977)

The explanation above is consistent with other studies that show both the importance of an event to an individual and its integration with other life events affect his reporting of them.

Table 2 can be examined for the presence of over- and underreporting of incidents connected with particular crime types. From this sample of offenders, robbery and rape were the most accurately reported. That is, relative to the other seven crime types considered, a higher percentage of the robbery- and rape-related incidents appearing on the rap sheets were also reported in the interviews. For robbery, the validity rate was 62%, and for rape, greater than 100% (rape was overreported by one conviction). Burglary and forgery also had relatively high validity rates—53%. The least accurately reported crime types were less serious offenses—grand larceny, aggravated assault, and auto theft.

Therefore, our results generally support the proposition that offenses that are less serious and less consequential for the offender will be less accurately reported.

By interview period. It is generally assumed that there is less error in reporting events that occurred in the recent than in the distant past. This is usually referred to as memory bias. However, there has been no research which tests this assumption when the information solicited concerns that of a criminal nature. It is plausible that when an offender is being asked about his criminal activities, he may be more likely to deny behaviors which occurred closest to the time of the interview. The offender's desire to appear rehabilitated in front of authorities may have conditioned many offenders to describe their behavior in such a way as to show a lessening of criminal activity or the recent adoption of legitimate life-styles. As such, the offender may be willing to accurately report his early criminal behavior, whereas he is more likely to deny recent criminality.

Since the interview was conducted in stages corresponding to contiguous time intervals, we can explore the "recency of events" theory. Table 2 presents the overall validity rates for the two adult periods. We would expect the information reported in the adult period to be more accurate than that from the young adult period, since

Table 2: Comparison of Self-Report Criminality Data with Official Records Data

Crime Type	Young Adult Period						Adult Period						Combined	
	Self-Reported Arrests	Rap Sheet Arrests	% Arrest Agreement[a]	Self-Reported Convictions	Rap Sheet Convictions	% Conviction Agreement[a]	Self-Reported Arrests	Rap Sheet Arrests	% Arrest Agreement	Self-Reported Convictions	Rap Sheet Convictions	% Conviction Agreement	% Arrest Agreement	% Conviction Agreement
Auto theft	9	24	37	5	16	31	1	3	33	1	2	50	37	33
Grand larceny	2	8	25	1	7	14	1	12	8	1	6	17	15	15
Burglary	19	58	33	15	23	65	4	18	22	2	9	22	30	53
Robbery	19	31	62	18	23	78	46	75	61	44	75	59	61	63
Aggravated assault	5	17	29[b]	2	7	28	0	9	0	0	5	0	19	17
Forgery	21	14	66[b]	15	11[b]	73	5	35	14[b]	4	25	16	53[b]	53[b]
Drug sales	3	1	33[b]	1	1	100[b]	4	0	0	2	0	0	14	33[b]
Rape	2	3	67	2	1	50[b]	1	1	100	1	1	100	75	67[b]
Total	80	156	(52)	59	89	(66)	62	153	(40)	55	123	(45)	(46)	(56)

a. % Arrest Agreement and % Conviction Agreement are defined as the percent of the arrests or convictions reported in the personal interview divided by the number appearing in the official rap sheet for the same interview period.

b. Indicates overreporting during the interview.

it was the time period closest to the interview. However, the results generally show the opposite. The arrest and conviction validity rates for the young adult period are 52% and 66%, respectively; corresponding rates for the adult period are 40% and 45%. Therefore, it is possible that the desire to look "rehabilitated" to the interviewer significantly affected the responses, perhaps more so than the offender's memory.

Gender of interviewer. Nearly every discussion in the literature about conducting interviews cautions about the biasing effects of the interviewer's gender. It is expected that a male or female interviewer will introduce unique forms of error, simply because the rapport established in the interview is likely to differ depending upon the sex of the respondent and the interviewer. Unfortunately, results concerning the direction of the error are inconsistent. Some researchers have shown that women interviewers tend to receive more puritanical and socially desirable answers from both men and women (Hyman et al., 1954; Colombotos et al., 1968; Cisin, 1965; Loewenstein and Varma, 1970). Other researchers have found women interviewers equally as effective as men interviewers (Pomeroy, 1963).

None of the just-cited studies on the effects of interviewer gender have dealt with interviews in which criminality data were solicited. Moreover, none of the respondents in the cited studies were incarcerated. Because this study solicited criminality data from prison inmates, we might expect the respondent/interviewer interaction to be more complex. Felons may be more concerned with presenting a "macho" image in front of other men; if so, they may exaggerate their criminal behavior. On the other hand, they may be anxious for approval, especially from women, so they may conceal their criminality in front of them. We explored these issues in our data.

Our interview staff consisted of three women and three men. All were white, similar in education level, socioeconomic status, and interview training. We compared the validity scores of the respondents interviewed by the men with those interviewed by the women. The average

Table 3: Validity Score by Interviewer Gender

Validity Score (%)	Interviewer Gender	
	Male (% of sample)	Female (% of sample)
26-50	36	27
51-75	52	68
76-100	12	5

a. The rates were calculated using all three interview periods.

validity of the former was 58%, of the latter, 57%. Analysis of the results by quartile groupings also revealed no significant differences in the validity scores. The results are presented in Table 3.

These findings suggest that this sample of incarcerated felons was equally truthful, whether they were being interviewed by a man or women.

Concluding Remarks

This chapter has reported on the crime rates of a group of offenders about whom there is particular concern in public policy—habitual felons. Resolution of current debates about the crime-reducing potential of incarcerating a greater percentage of such persons for longer terms hinges on estimates of the amount of crime they actually commit and their probability of arrest and conviction. This study provides just such estimates, by crime type and period in the criminal career, based on the offenders' own reports.

Moreover, the study assessed the validity of such reports by comparing the interview responses with official records data. The results show that, on the average, respondents reported approximately 50% of either their official arrests or convictions during the interviews. The percentage increased to 75% if juvenile events were included. Furthermore, contrary to expectations, there was less validity associated with the reporting of *less* serious offenses and with events occurring *closest* to the time of the interview.

Since it is apparent that self-reported methods will be more popular as a means for assessing the extent of a person's criminal behavior, it is necessary that more attention be paid to the methodological problems in their use. This study represents just a beginning. In the next two years, Rand Corporation will be refining and improving the interview procedures utilized in this study. Alternative methods of cross-checking data for validity will be explored. Different samples of offenders will be drawn, such as burglars or juvenile felons, to examine whether the results reported here, concerning a relatively small and select sample, can be duplicated.

NOTES

1. The Reference section lists previous studies which have attempted to assess the extent of a population's deviant behavior through self-reports, and also report on the validity of the information obtained. The majority of these deal with juvenile populations.

2. In 1975, the Rand Corporation was awarded a grant under the Research Agreements Program (RAP) of the National Institute of Law Enforcement and Criminal Justice. The grant provided funding for a variety of research projects addressed to serious habitual offenders. The results from this particular project are reported in *Criminal Careers of Habitual Felons* (Rand Corporation, R-2144, July 1977).

3. A pretest of the interview instrument indicated that these nine offense types not only constituted a large proportion of the serious and not-so-serious offenses committed, but also spanned both juvenile and adult crime as well as property and personal offenses.

4. The criminal career length was measured from time of first recorded arrest (rather than first self-reported offense). Percent-at-risk street time/(street time plus incarceration time) was calculated using the offender's statements concerning the length he served upon each conviction.

REFERENCES

BALL, J. C. (1967) "The reality and validity of interview data obtained from 59 narcotic drug addicts." Amer. J. of Sociology 72: 650-654.

CISIN, I. (1965) An Experimental Study of Sensitivity of Survey Techniques in Measuring Drinking Practices. George Washington University, Social Research Project.

*CLARK, J. P. and L. L. TIFFT (1966) "Polygraph and interview validation of self reported deviant behavior." Amer. Soc. Rev. 31: 516-523.

COLOMBOTOS, J., J. ELINSON, and R. LOEWENSTEIN (1968) "Effect of interviewers' sex on interview responses." Public Health Reports 8: 685-690.

ERICKSON, M. (1972) "The changing relationship between official and self-reported delinquency." J. of Criminal Law, Criminology and Police Sci. 63 (September): 388-395.

——— and L. T. EMPEY (1963) "Court records, undetected delinquency and decision making." J. of Criminal Law, Criminology and Police Sci. 54: 456-469.

FARRINGTON, D. P. (1973) "Self-reports of deviant behavior: predictive and stable." J. of Criminal Law, Criminology and Police Sci. 641: 99-110.

*——— and D. WEST (1971) "A comparison between early delinquents and young aggressives." British J. of Criminology 11: 341-358.

*GOLD, M. (1966) "Undetected delinquent behavior." J. of Research in Crime and Delinquency 3: 27-46.

*GOULD, L. C. (1969) "Who defines delinquency: a comparison of self-report and officially-reported indices of delinquency for three racial groups." Social Problems 16: 325-336.

*HACKLEY, J. C. and M. LAUTT (1969) "Systematic bias in measuring self-reported delinquency." Canadian Rev. of Sociology and Anthropology 6: 92-106.

*HARDT, R. H. and S. J. PETERSON (1968) "Neighborhood status and delinquency activity as indexed by policy records and a self-report survey." Criminologica 6: 37-47.

HOOD, R. and R. SPARKS (1973) Key Issues in Criminology. New York: Cambridge Univ. Press.

HYMAN, H. H., W. J. COBB, J. J. FELDMAN, C. W. HART, and C. H. STEMBER (1954) Interviewing in Social Research. Chicago: Univ. of Chicago Press.

*KAPLAN, H. (1976) "Self attitudes and deviant response." Social Forces 54: 788-801.

*KULICK, J., K. STEIN, T. SARBIN (1968) "Dimensions and patterns of adolescent antisocial behavior." J. of Consulting and Clinical Psychology 32: 378.

POMEROY, W. B. (1963) "The reluctant respondent." Public Opinion Q. 27: 287-293.

TIELMAN, K. (1977) "Self-report criminality and interviewer effects." Ph.D. dissertation, University of Southern California.

*WALSH, B. W. (1967) "Validity of self-report." J. of Counseling Psychology 14: 18-23.

NOTE: The asterisks indicate studies which attempt to assess the validity of the self-reported criminality information.

Deborah M. Galvin
University of Pennsylvania

3

THE SERIOUSNESS
OF OFFENSES:
An Evaluation of Children
and Adolescents

Current literature in the field of criminology has given little attention to the child's perception of criminal offenses. This chapter will explore the developmental patterns involved in children and adolescents' determination of the subjective severities of various kinds of criminal offenses including status offenses. Further, this report aims to determine the chronological age at which children and/or adolescents begin to rank the seriousness of crime in the same manner as do adults with regard to offense ranking, weight given to each offense, and the degree of consensus about the seriousness of each offense. Other issues will be addressed, such as when is a child able to know the severity and absoluteness of a homicide, is there a difference between chronological ages of ranking particular types of crime events as more or less serious, and what are the differences between chronological ages of how children and youth rank crimes against the person as compared to property offenses.

Child development theory and specifically cognitive-developmental theory of moral development not only served as a foundation on which to build the research design, but also aided in the interpretation of the data. As the subject of perception can be placed in the domain of "morality," theories of development of moral judgement are conse-

AUTHOR'S NOTE: This investigation was supported by the alcohol, drug abuse, and mental health administration, National Research Award, Grant Number 5-F-31-MH-05889, from the National Institute of Mental Health, Rockville, Maryland. This paper was presented at the American Society of Criminology at Atlanta, Georgia, November 17-20, 1977.

quential in this analysis. Major stage theories of Piaget (1948, 1954), Freud (1949), Erikson (1950) and Kohlberg (1964, 1971) have influenced the literature significantly. However, theories concerned with moral development have given little or no attention to defining morality. Theorists and researchers have assumed that their measuring tools and analyses constituted a valid representation of "morality," although these representations have not been complete. Concepts of morality have neglected the individual's perception of the nature of morality and law as well as the extent to which incidents are considered to be moral problems. The assumption is then made that this research is pertinent to moral developmental theory.

As the word "morality" has been used to a great extent in the literature, and there is agreement to its adequacy, it will be used in this study as well. Clearly, this chapter is not concerned with morality as a theological construct. Rather, "morality" will be used loosely to denote some form of social harm or benefit or in terms of what is "right or wrong." As the offenses used to scale seriousness are against the law, there is some amount of societal agreement that they do cause some amount of social harm and are "wrong." For these reasons, morality literature applies to this study.

Severity of crime events can be seen in terms of a measurement of the amount of perceived social harm created by particular incidents. The assumption that certain crimes are more serious than others and that adults are able to discriminate between the various crimes as to the differences in severity can be made from findings reported in *The Measurement of Delinquency* by Sellin and Wolfgang (1964). Although the purpose of their research was to develop a scale of seriousness of crime to measure more efficiently the incidence of delinquency, its most important result for this research was that adults do discriminate between various crime events and that there is a consensus among adults as to severity of crime.

In order to determine the patterns involved with children developing crime severity discrimination abilities, a validated scale to measure "severity" of crime was necessary.

The Sellin-Wolfgang scale of seriousness of crime served this purpose. The original methods used in formulating the index were based on the work of Stevens (1966) in the field of psychophysical scaling. (Psychophysical scaling is a technique used to discriminate between nonphysical continua, such as noise level or loudness, and, in this case, seriousness of crime.)

The original Sellin-Wolfgang study compiled a list of 141 offenses involving acts of injury, theft, and/or damage from a review of case records from the Philadelphia Police Juvenile Aid Division for the year 1960. With the use of a magnitude estimation scale and a category (interval) scale, similar results were produced along a continuum by the scoring of judges. The final scale was produced with the scores of 195 university students and consisted of the twenty offenses to be used in this research. Replications of this study have used different sets of "adult" judges and have shown similar results (including Normandeau [1966], Akman et al. [1967], Hsu [1973], and Figlio [1975]). This scale was then chosen as the metric to rate seriousness of crime as it was both convenient and validated. Indeed, it measured the severity of juvenile offenses including status offenses as found in police records, and was thus ideal for this research.

The Pretest

It was necessary to modify the original stimuli from the Sellin-Wolfgang scale for use by juvenile judges. With knowledge from previous child developmental research and a pilot testing period, this task was accomplished. The purpose of the pretest was to aid in the modification of the scale and to encounter any difficulties which were necessary to handle before the actual sampling. The pretest process involved an in-depth interviewing process with 59 children and adolescents ages 4 through 12 from a mixture of nationalities, sex, race, and class backgrounds.

Several alterations essential to obtaining accurate and valid reponses included simplifications of sentence structuring, vocabulary, instructions, and scaling technique. The decision was made to use a modified Sellin-Wolfgang category scale with several changes (e.g., the word "offender" was replaced by "a person") and a simplified 10-event category scale developed with a scaled 11-story house for the younger children, grades Kindergarten through third grade (ages 4-8).

The pretest stage detected that younger children had a shorter attention span and therefore needed to have instructions repeated several times with each new stimuli. Further, they were unable to respond to as many items as older youth. As the majority of youth were unable to master the magnitude estimation scale until the ages of 10-12, a category scaling technique was chosen. In addition, younger children were unable to fathom a line representation of the category scale although it was possible to use a drawing of a house with floors drawn to scale representing the intervals. Phrases such as "a person takes $5 worth of property" were perplexing to many of the younger children as were a variety of terms such as "rape," "forced sexual intercourse," "offender," "victim," "prowling," and "rifle."

The Sample

The sample was obtained from a public school system in a Mid-Atlantic cosmopolitan area. The public school system indicated which schools and classes the interviewers were able to enter, and permission forms were obtained from all parents of children involved in the research along with the approval of all participants. Ten of the 42 schools in the system were selected for the survey. Two schools were chosen per grade category and were selected for the widest range between socioeconomic backgrounds. Several classes per school were used to obtain a 30-student per class per school minimum.

A representative sampling was difficult to obtain due to variations caused by the absence of "residential area" schools created by city-wide busing for desegregation purposes and lack of any universal regulations concerning placement of youth into classrooms. There were also a number of specifications and regulations which had to be met in order to obtain entrance into the school system, such as permissible subject matter, time limitations, and scheduling.

The older youth (4-12 grades) received a booklet (8½ x 5¼) listing offense events to be ranked on an 11-point category scale. The first page of the booklet contained background information of each student (age, grade in school, and sex). No names were recorded since each rater was to remain anonymous. Additional pages of the booklet contained the offense events, one per page, and sequentially numbered according to one of four color-coded random forms. The random forms were assembled with the use of a random numbers table which was necessary to prevent an ordering effect. On the bottom of each page was a drawn 11-point scale. An example (in reduced form) is as follows:

1. A person disturbs the neighborhood with loud, noisy behavior.

1	2	3	4	5	6	7	8	9	10	11

not serious
or
important

serious
or
important

Each testing situation was treated similarly to a scheduled interview. Both the instructions and introduction and the interviewer and assistant remained the same throughout the sampling period. Based on growing reports in educational journals that there are a large number of graduating high school students without sufficient reading comprehension, it was necessary to read each item at least twice before students responded to the event. This avoided any contamination of the data and increased the validity of the responses.

A sample of 97 students from a number of classes in a Mid-Altantic State university were representative of the "adult" population as found in the Sellin-Wolfgang research where students were assumed to have "typical middle-class values," and results from this original study and replications confirmed the assumption. This research also assumes that the university sample is representative of "typical middle-class adult values." The necessity for drawing a new sampling from a university was completed as a protective measure to prevent any variation in comparisons between a youth and an "adult" population which may have occurred over time (between the Sellin-Wolfgang study, replications, and this research) and to insure that modifications made for this research did not affect the final outcome. The university students received all four forms of the booklet used for the older youth. Instructions were not repeated as many times as for the juvenile population and all college students were assumed to have the ability to read the booklets by themselves and respond to each event without additional reading from the interviewer.

Analysis of the Results

The following is a list of the events which the younger children (Kindergarten through third grade) responded to.

(1) A person takes (steals) a crayon from the school's supply box.

(2) A person your age skips or plays hookey from school and is caught.

(3) A person your age runs away from home and is caught.

(4) A person walks into your house when no one is there and steals your favorite toys. (Compares with older children's event concerning $5 worth of property.)

(5) A person without a gun threatens to hurt you unless you give him your favorite toys. You give him your favorite toys and he does not hurt you.

(6) A person breaks into your house, comes in and steals your favorite toys. (Compares with older children's event concerning $5 worth of property.)

(7) A person walks into your house when no one is there and steals the television and radio. (Compares with $1,000 worth of property on the older children's form.)

(8) A person with a gun threatens to hurt you unless you give him your favorite toys. You give him your favorite toys and he does not hurt you.

(9) One person hurts another who has to go to a hospital to be treated or helped.

(10) One person hurts another who dies from the injury.

These events were compared to similar (not equivalent) events from the older group (see Appendix A for listing of the older group's events). Exact replications were not possible in the younger grades due to lack of comprehension and span of attention (as explained earlier). Regarding the analysis and findings, it is necessary to specify that there are difficulties involved with the validity of the comparison between the two groups (younger and older), although general trends between the groups are possible to ascertain. Thus, the results in the larger study are analyzed with two sets of data. The first set (to be examined here) is composed of grades Kindergarten through college comparing the 10 events for the younger children to a corresponding set for the older children/adolescents and control set of "adults." The second set of data analyzes the complete list of the 25-event items as judged by grades 4 through college.

The results from the present study provide evidence that as children mature, there is an increased ability to discriminate between crime events placing the most serious at one end of the scale and minor offenses at the lower end. Inspection of Figure 1 (the mean severity scores) reveals that, in general, the younger children respond more seriously to events than do older youth/adults. We find that there is much more agreement in ordering of events for grades 7-12 and college than for the younger grades. Further, there appears to be an even greater similarity between adjacent grades than between a higher and lower grade.

Table 1 shows that all of the correlations of a younger grade (X) with an older grade (Y) are positive and that there is a general tendency for grade levels in close proximity to have a high correlation. As the distance between the grade level increases, there is also a tendency for the correlation to decrease. In other words, with few exceptions, as the distance between grades increases, typically the scatter in the path of the mean scores increases and the goodness of the fit decreases. Thus there is a strong linear relationship between Kindergarten and first, second, and third grades, and so on with a decreasing linear relationship between Kindergarten and fourth grade and a slight linear relationship between Kindergarten and grade 12 or college.

RESPONSE BY GRADE

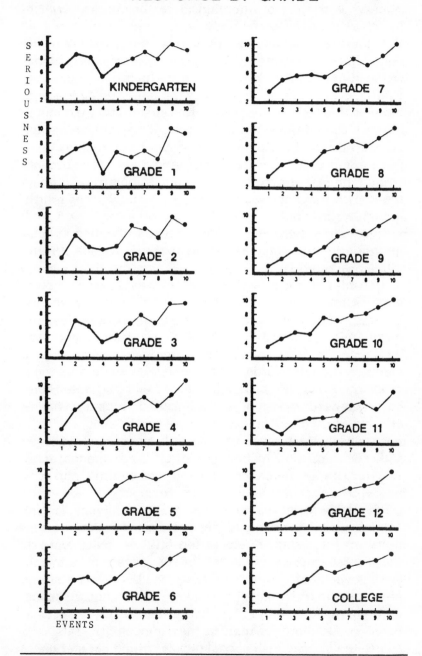

Figure 1

These findings indicate that there is no one particular point-in-time in which a child learns to discriminate on severity of crime, or any magical cut-off point at which the child develops a finalized perception of crime. It is only possible to state that youth around grades 7-8 (ages 13-15) begin to rate severity of crime with an even greater similarity to adults than do younger children.

Referring to Figure 1 again, it is observed that some property offenses are considered more serious than some crimes against the person. Grades 4-college rated homicide as the most serious offense, whereas Kindergarten-third grade rated stealing a television and radio as the most serious offense (more serious than a homicide or any other crime against the person). In addition, the fourth and eleventh grades rated stealing of a television and radio as being more serious than assault resulting in hospitalization of the victim as the second most serious offense following homicide.

The ordering for property offenses was upward in seriousness for larceny of favorite toys/$5 and burglary of favorite toys/$5 and downward in seriousness for larceny of the television and radio/$1,000 as grade increased. For crimes against the person, there appeared to be a shifting but upward ordering for robbery without a weapon of favorite toys/$5 which began in the eighth grade. There was increased rating of seriousness of robbery with a weapon which was gradual in nature and by seventh grade most closely resembled the twelfth grade and college. With the exception of first grade, all other grades rated robbery without a weapon as being less serious than robbery with a weapon as would be expected.

The status offenses of skipping school (Event 2) and running away from home (Event 3) are rated as very serious by younger grades (Kindergarten-fifth or sixth grades), and less serious by the older grades (seventh grade-college). In addition, running away from home is rated as more severe than skipping school. There appears to be more agreement within the older grades as to the severity of the status offenses than in the younger grades.

Taking a crayon from school (not returning library books, grades 4-college) was rated as either the least serious

Table 1: Pearson Correlations of Mean Seriousness Scores for Younger Grades (X) With Older Grades (Y)

GRADES (X and Y)	TOTAL OBSERVATIONS	PEARSON CORRELATIONS
Kindergarten & 1	113	r = .8838
1 & 2	110	r = .6429
2 & 3	112	r = .9333
3 & 4	114	r = .8314
4 & 5	110	r = .9519
5 & 6	116	r = .9543
6 & 7	133	r = .9501
7 & 8	151	r = .9488
8 & 9	151	r = .9803
9 & 10	122	r = .9663
10 & 11	121	r = .8492
11 & 12	132	r = .9083
12 & College	165	r = .9853
Kindergarten & 1	113	r = .8838
K & 2	123	r = .8110
K & 3	112	r = .8889
K & 4	125	r = .7761
K & 12	131	r = .5088
K & College	160	r = .4108
Kindergarten & 12	131	r = .5088
1 & 12	118	r = .4012
2 & 12	128	r = .7504
3 & 12	120	r = .7106
4 & 12	130	r = .7776
5 & 12	116	r = .8165
6 & 12	136	r = .8966
7 & 12	133	r = .9224
8 & 12	154	r = .9754
9 & 12	133	r = .9647
10 & 12	125	r = .9931
11 & 12	132	r = .9251
College & 12	165	r = .9881
Kindergarten & College	160	r = .4108
1 & College	147	r = .3299
2 & College	157	r = .6984
3 & College	149	r = .6386
4 & College	159	r = .7066
5 & College	145	r = .7372
6 & College	165	r = .8337
7 & College	162	r = .8796
8 & College	183	r = .9410
9 & College	162	r = .9241
10 & College	154	r = .9799
11 & College	161	r = .9231
12 & College	165	r = .9881

Table 2: Population by Grade

GRADE	POPULATION
Kindergarten	63
1	50
2	60
3	52
4	62
5	48
6	68
7	65
8	86
9	65
10	57
11	64
12	68
College	97

offense or the second least serious offense for most grades as compared to the other offenses. In addition, grades Kindergarten-sixth grade rated larceny of favorite toys/ $5 as either least serious or the second least serious offense, while grades 7-college rated skipping school as the least serious or second least serious offense.

What is obvious from the data reported here is that children at age 4 or older are able to perceive crime events as serious. Although there is a tendency to discriminate with a wider range of sense of severity for older youth, all children, adolescents, and adults did discriminate between the various offenses. Beginning with the seventh-eighth grades (ages 13-15), the graphs indicating mean severity response for the 10 events appeared to have a greater similarity to the responses given by high school students and the control group, college. There was a high correlation between students in adjacent grades which tended to decrease as the gap between the grade levels increased. In addition, there was less consensus on the ordering of crime events in the younger grades than the older grades.

Discussion

There are a number of plausible explanations for the findings. Crime severity discrimination development might be more of a social learning process in the age groups tested so that the most significant variables operating might be experiential ones. The child relates more to crime events he has had some experience with rather than crime events he may have heard about. Thus, stealing the television and radio might be ranked as more serious than a homicide in Kindergarten-third grade because homicide does not have the same sense of reality to him/her. The child might know the meaning of the concept "death" denotatively (its socially accepted definition) but not connotatively (its emotional and evaluative meaning). What the word "death" means to a child connotatively might not be the same as it appears to an older child. Although the child may have some notion of "death," he/she may not have as many experiences with it to attach an emotional content (such as sadness, anger, fear) to it. As the child matures, he/she attaches more symbols to the word "death." Perhaps as the number of symbols and patterns of experience attached to the stimulus word "homicide" or "death" increases so does the severity of the event.

Likewise for other offenses, the ability to discriminate among them similar to adults might be related to the experience of the child and how the child perceives the rest of society around him. The younger child might rate status offenses more seriously than do older children due to perceived self-survival. The younger child is quite dependent upon the adult for survival with the peer group not as relevant for self-concept at this stage. As the child matures, he gains self-actualization and peer group becomes more relevant. As this occurs, the severity of status offenses decreases. The child begins to label himself more in terms of being equivalent to an adult with the status offense as a threat to this freedom. As the child gains personal power and more personal freedoms, the perceived severity of status offenses decreases.

Another explanation would be that as the child matures, he is more capable of placing status offenses in perspective with other offenses and views them as being more arbitrary with less social harm created by committing them. We might find that perception of crime develops along with perception of other belief systems, abilities, and attitudes. Similar to Damon's (1977) findings, it is possible that crime severity discrimination is associated with the acquisition of social knowledge concerning positive justice, parental and peer authority, social regulation, spatial perspective, and social perspective.

From the data collected, it is only possible to speculate as to the reasons that the younger children tend to rank all crime as very serious and as age increased, there is a widening of discrimination between the various offenses. Both cognitive developmental theories and learning theories give plausible explanations for these results.

The results have mixed implications to the question of "responsibility." If the child/adolescent is unable to perceive crime severity in a similar fashion as adults, should he/she be held responsible for his/her actions? In addition, if the individual is capable of discriminating between the various types of crimes similar to an adult population, it may not follow that the individual comprehends the severity of the offense he/she committed. We can also study whether there is a relationship between ability to discriminate between crime events and involvement of juveniles in delinquency and crime.

Summary

The process in which children/adolescents come to view the seriousness of crime and at what point they are capable of understanding the severity of their actions is an important dimension of child development and criminological research which was neglected in the past. The Sellin-Wolfgang seriousness scale was indispensable to this study as a metric to rate seriousness of crime. The findings pose further questions to be explored in future research and may aid in the search for understanding delinquency. In future research other techniques and replications of this technique might be used to probe into the many issues this research has raised as well as new conceptualizations of the problem.

REFERENCES

AKMAN, D., A. NORMANDEAU, and S. TURNER (1967) "The Measurement of delinquency in Canada." J. of Criminal Law, Criminology and Police Sciences 58: 339-337.

ARLIN, P. K. (1975) "Cognitive development in adulthood: a fifth stage?" Developmental Psychology 2: 602-606.

BANDURA, A. and F. J. McDONALD (1969) "Influence of social reinforcement and the behavior of models in shaping children's moral judgments," pp. 57-71 in H. C. Lindgren (ed.) Contemporary Research in Social Psychology. New York: John Wiley.

BERG-CROSS, L. (1975) "Intentionality, degree of damage and moral judgments." Child Development 46: 970-974.

BERNDT, T. and E. BERNDT (1975) "Children's use of motives and intentionality in person perception and moral judgment." Child Development 46: 904-912.

BRIDGES, G. S. and N. S. LISAGOR (1975) "Scaling seriousness: an evaluation of magnitude and category scaling techniques." J. of Criminal Law and Criminology 65: 215-221.

CHANDLER, M. J., S. GREENSPAN, and C. BARENBOIM (1973) "Judgments of intentionality in response to videotaped and verbally presented moral dilemmas: the medium is the message." Child Development 44: 315-320.

DAMON, W. (1977) The Social World of the Child. San Francisco: Jossey-Bass.

ERIKSON, E. (1950) Childhood and Society. New York: W. W. Norton.

FELDMAN, N. S., E. C. KLOSSON, J. E. PARSONS, W. S. RHOLES, and D. N. RUBLE (1976) "Order of information presentation and children's moral judgments." Child Development 47: 556-559.

FIGLIO, R. M. (1975) "The seriousness of offenses: an evaluation by offenders and nonoffenders." J. of Criminal Law and Criminology 66: 189-200.

FREUD, S. (1949) An Outline of Psychoanalysis. New York: W. W. Norton.

GUTKIN, D. C. (1972) "The effect of systematic story changes on intentionality in children's moral judgments." Child Development 43: 187-195.

HSU, M. (1973) "Cultural and sexual differences in the judgment of criminal offenses." J. of Criminal Law and Criminology 64: 348.

KOHLBERG, L. (1971) "From is to ought," in T. Mischel (ed.) Cognitive Development and Epistemology. New York: Academic Press.

——— (1969) "Stage and sequence: the cognitive-developmental approach to socialization theory and research. New York: Rand McNally.

——— (1964) "Development of moral character and ideology," in M. L. Hoffman and L.N.W. Hoffman (eds.) Review of Child Development Research, Vol. 1. New York: Russell Sage Foundation.

NORMANDEAU, A. (1966) "The measurement of delinquency in Montreal." J. of Criminology and Criminal Law 57: 172.

PARSONS, J. E., D. N. RUBLE, E. C. KLOSSON, N. S. FELDMAN, and W. S. RHOLES (1976) "Order effects on children's moral and achievement judgments." Developmental Psychology 12: 357-358.

PIAGET, J. (1954) The Construction of Reality in the Child. New York: Basic Books.

——— (1948) The Moral Judgment of the Child. New York: Free Press.

REST, J. R. (1975) "Longitudinal study of the defining issues test of moral judg-
ment: a strategy for analyzing developmental change." Developmental Psy-
chology 2: 738-748.
SELLIN, T. and M. E. WOLFGANG (1964) The Measurement of Delinquency.
New York: John Wiley.
STEVENS, S. (1966) "A metric for the social consensus." Sci. 151: 530.
SYKES, G. and D. MATZA (1957) "Techniques of neutralization: a theory of delin-
quency." Amer. Soc. Rev. 22: 644-670.
WELLFORD, C. F. (1975) "On the measurement of delinquency." J. of Criminal
Law and Criminology 66: 175-188.

APPENDIX A

LIST OF TWENTY-FIVE EVENTS FOR GRADES 4-COLLEGE

(1) A person takes $5 worth of property. It was done by the person alone, and the person did not break into or enter a building.

(2) A person takes $20 worth of property. It was done by the person alone, and the person did not break into or enter a building.

(3) A person takes $50 worth of property. It was done by the person alone, and the person did not break into or enter a building.

(4) A person takes $1,000 worth of property. It was done by the person alone, and the person did not break into or enter a building.

(5) A person takes $5,000 worth of property. It was done by the person alone, and the person did not break into or enter a building.

(6) A person takes $5 worth of property. It was done by the person alone, and the person broke into a building.

(7) A person without a weapon threatens to hurt another person (the victim) unless the victim gives him money. The person takes the victim's money ($5) and leaves without hurting the victim.

(8) A person with a weapon threatens to hurt another person (the victim) unless the victim gives him money. The person takes the victim's money ($5) and leaves without hurting the victim.

(9) A person injures another person (the victim). The victim dies from the injury.

(10) A person injures another person (the victim). The victim is treated by a doctor and his injuries require him to be hospitalized.

(11) A person injures another person (the victim). The victim is treated by a doctor but his injuries do not require him to be hospitalized.

(12) A person shoves or pushes a victim. The victim does not require any medical treatment.

(13) A male forces a female to submit to sexual intercourse (rape). There is no other injury done.

(14) A person takes an automobile which is recovered undamaged.

(15) A person is found firing a gun for which he/she has no permit.

(16) A person prowls in the backyard of a private residence.

(17) A person is a customer in a place where liquor is sold illegally.

(18) A person disturbs the neighborhood with loud, noisy behavior.

(19) A person under age runs away from home and thereby becomes an offender.

(20) A person under age plays hookey from school and thereby becomes an offender.

(21) A person working in a store does not put all of the customer's money into the cash box and keeps $50 of it for himself/herself.

(22) A person who works at a bank takes $1,000 of the bank's money home without anyone knowing.

(23) A person who works at a bank takes $5,000 of the bank's money home without anyone knowing.

(24) A person cheats on an exam (test) in the math class.

(25) A person does not return his/her books to the library.

Charles Logan
University of Connecticut

4

STATISTICAL ARTIFACTS IN DETERRENCE RESEARCH

THE IMPACT OF DETERRENCE RESEARCH

For a long time in the history of social science, it did not appear to matter much whether social scientists were right or wrong. Their ideas and research were not of such influence as to make vital the careful scrutiny of their validity. Now, however, there are instances of social science testimony or research whose relevance to some explosive political issue generates a greater need for more critical evaluation than might otherwise have been called for.

It may be arguable whether research on the deterrent effects of legal sanctions has had that strong an impact on public policy, but if it has not yet, the potential is still there. Public concern with crime is extremely high. Debates over the deterrent effectiveness of capital punishment are being revived, both in general and before the Supreme Court, where specific research on that topic has been presented in

AUTHOR'S NOTE: Paper presented to American Society of Criminology, Atlanta, Georgia, November 17, 1977. The research was supported in part by NIMH (Grant #MH 24574-01) and the University of Connecticut Research Foundation. Computer time was provided by the University of Connecticut Computer Center. Karl Schuessler and Robert Weber were most helpful at certain stages of the paper's development but cannot be held responsible for any deficiencies in its final form.

briefs. Criminal justice policy analysts have been shifting their focus away from rehabilitation and toward retribution, justice, incapacitation, and deterrence (American Friends Service Committee, 1971; Morris, 1974; Wilson, 1975; Von Hirsch, 1976). Criminal justice research has reflected this same shift of focus, particularly in the burgeoning of research on deterrence. Although all scientific research deserves critical evaluation, the current growth and potential policy influence of deterrence research indicates that careful scrutiny is particularly important in this area.

THE PROBLEM OF SPURIOUS RATIO CORRELATIONS IN DETERRENCE RESEARCH

In critiques of deterrence research thus far, relatively little attention has been paid to one very basic difficulty common to much of this research. The early core of deterrence research consisted of a group of studies that discovered a remarkably consistent negative relationship between crime rate and some measure of certainty of criminal sanction (punishment) for crime. These studies all used cross-sectional data aggregated by state, county, and city units. The sanctions they dealt with were *execution* (Schuessler, 1952; Ehrlich, 1975), *imprisonment* (Gibbs, 1968; Tittle, 1969; Gray and Martin, 1969; Chiricos and Waldo, 1970; Bailey et al., 1971; Bean and Cushing, 1971; Kobrin et al., 1972; Logan, 1972; Ehrlich, 1972, 1973; Antunes and Hunt, 1973; Erickson and Gibbs, 1973; Vandaele, 1976), and *arrest* (Kobrin et al., 1973; Block, 1972; Phillips and Votey, 1972; Chapman, 1973; Tittle and Rowe, 1974; Logan, 1975). Thus, units with higher rates of punishment (arrest, imprisonment, or execution) tended to show lower rates of crime, and vice versa.

The problem common to these studies consists of a possible definitional dependency, or contamination, between the measures of the independent and dependent variables. The independent variable, certainty of sanction, consists of the ratio of sanctions to crimes, denoted here as A/C. ("A" is used because in most studies the sanction is admission to prison or arrest.) The dependent variable is per capita crime rate, denoted as C/P. The common term, C, has been either identical or very highly correlated between the two ratios in the data analyzed by the studies described above.

When two ratios containing a common term are correlated, there is always a question of whether the correlation might be a spurious mathematical artifact of the common term. In the deterrence research, the common term, C, might tend to simultaneously deflate the value of A/C and inflate the value of C/P. If so, this would produce a negative correlation, which would be in the same direction as the relation predicted by deterrence theory.

Accordingly, this chapter focuses only on the question of whether the negative correlations repeatedly found between certainty of sanction and crime rates can be accounted for by some kind of "indexical artifice" resulting from the way in which these two variables are measured in the literature cited above. One data set from this literature (Logan, 1972) will be used for illustration throughout this chapter. This set consists of data on rates of crime and imprisonment. The intent, however, is not to question any one particular set of findings. Rather, the point is to discuss a problem common to many, if not most, deterrence studies, with one data set used for consistency of illustration and demonstration.

RESPONSES TO THE PROBLEM OF SPURIOUSNESS IN RATIO CORRELATION

The problem of correlating ratios having common terms has been addressed specifically in the deterrence literature (Tittle, 1969; Logan, 1971, 1972, 1975; Chiricos and Waldo, 1970) as well as in more general methodological literature (Pearson, 1897; Schuessler, 1973, 1974; Fuguitt and Lieberson, 1974; Freeman and Kronenfeld, 1973). Several alternative resolutions that have been suggested will be critically examined. These are: (1) the "theoretical-meaning" resolution, (2) the Pearsonian approximation formula and null comparison, (3) simulation techniques, (4) decomposition into component covariances, and (5) part correlation and the use of residual scores.

Theoretical Primacy of the Ratios

One early and continuing disclaimer has been that if our primary theoretical interest is in the ratios per se, rather than in the components that make up the ratios, then the issue of spuriousness in the correlation of two ratios does not logically arise, even if they do have a common term (Pearson, 1897; Yule, 1910; Kuh and Meyer, 1955; Rangarajan and Chatterjee, 1969; McNemar, 1969: 181; Schuessler, 1973: 217; Fuguitt and Lieberson, 1974: 132). An analogy could be made to the well-known positive association between speed (miles per hour) and gas consumption (gallons per mile), where we are also not interested in the relation among the components but in the relation between the ratios. In this example, it is clear that the ratio variables are not mere epiphenomena, created by the artifact of dividing one measurement by another, but are theoretically meaningful variables in themselves. Further, we expect these ratios to be causally related to each other in a manner relatively independent of the way in which the components vary separately, and opposite in sign to what would be expected as a result of "indexical artifact."

However, the theoretical rationale behind a given ratio index may not always be as clear in sociology as it sometimes is in physics, or a ration may stand as a proxy measure for some more immediately causal, but not directly measurable variable. In deterrence research, for example, there is a clear theoretical rationale for measuring the proportion of crimes that result in apprehension and punishment, but it is not so obvious that such measures will be valid when they are constructed from questionable official statistics. In addition, it can be shown for some data that even when two theoretically meaningful ratios correlate in the direction predicted by theory, it is also possible to achieve a similar correlation when the ratios are reconstructed using randomized or scrambled values for the components. This will be explained below. In this situation we may be at an interpretive impasse: while the empirical correlation is theoretically meaningful, it cannot be shown to be different from one that would result if the data were randomized or scrambled, in which case the ratios and their correlation would be theoretically meaningless. Such a situation—which will be shown to exist with the imprisonment data—would contain no clear implication for the validity of the empirical correlations. Still, it would at least suggest that the issue of artifactuality ought not to be dismissed purely on logical grounds.

The Pearsonian Null Comparison

In perhaps the earliest treatment of this problem, Pearson (1897) developed a formula giving an approximation of the correlation between two ratios in terms of the correlations and rel-variances (or coefficients of variation) of the component terms. For the case of A/C and C/P Pearson's formula would be:

$$r_{(A/C)(C/P)} = \frac{r_{AC}V_AV_C - r_{AP}V_AV_P - V_C^2 + r_{CP}V_CV_P}{\sqrt{V_A^2 + V_C^2 - 2r_{AC}V_AV_C}\sqrt{V_C^2 + V_P^2 - 2r_{CP}V_CV_P}}. \quad [1]$$

The most commonly suggested (Pearson, 1897; Yule, 1910; Yule and Kendall, 1950; Kuh and Meyer, 1955; Rangarajan and Chatterjee, 1969; Chayes, 1971; Fuguitt and Lieberson, 1974) approach to the problem of spuriousness in ratio correlation involves a manipulation of formula 1 to produce a null value representing the correlation between A/C and C/P that would be expected to occur under the condition that the components (A, C, and P) are uncorrelated. If $r_{AC} = r_{CP} = r_{AP} = 0$, formula 1 becomes:

$$\frac{-V_C^2}{\sqrt{V_A^2 + V_C^2} \ \sqrt{V_C^2 + V_P^2}} \tag{2}$$

a value that will obviously be negative. Pearson referred to this value as the "spurious correlation," while Chayes refers to it as the "null correlation." Comparing the values computed by formulas 1 and 2 is supposed to be analogous to a test of the ordinary null hypothesis that r = 0. Thus, an empirical correlation larger than the value from formula 2 would be needed to reject the null hypothesis of a nonartifactual correlation between the ratios.

Strictly speaking, however, the null comparison does not directly test the hypothesis of noncorrelation between two ratios; rather it tests the hypothesis of noncorrelation among the *components,* which is only one condition that would produce noncorrelation between the ratios. Finding a correlation larger than the test value, and thus rejecting the null hypothesis, should therefore only mean rejection of the assumption that the *components* are uncorrelated in the population. We cannot reject the possibility that the ratios may still be correlated only as a function of the common term, because we do not know how strong that artifactual correlation would be under the different condition of correlated components.

In our sample data (and therefore, by statistical inference, in the population), the correlations among the components will either be unknown, known to be zero, or known to be nonzero. If the component correlations in the sample are unknown (a situation that is probably extremely rare in sociological research), a ratio correlation significantly greater than the null value would tell us that the components must in fact be correlated in the population. This might be useful new information, but there is a paradox in this situation: in order to apply formulas 1 and 2 we must already know the means and variances of the components, and if we know those we will almost certainly also have the data needed to compute the intercorrelation of the components.

If we know from the sample data that the components are not correlated, then the ratio correlation computed by formula 1 will of necessity be exactly the same as the null correlation computed by formula 2—hence the test will be unnecessary.

On the other hand, if the three components of two ratios are known to be correlated, what can be concluded from a comparison of the empirical and null correlations of the ratios? Only that the empirical correlation is less than, equal to, or greater than what would result from indexical artifice under conditions known not to exist.

In sum, it is not clear (to me) that Pearson's null comparison can properly be used to test for the operation of a common term in the two ratios.

Simulation Techniques

It is important to note that because Pearson's basic formula was derived from a binomial expansion in which terms higher than the second order were dropped, it is an approximation that becomes subject to serious error when any of the values of V rise above 0.15 (Chayes, 1971: 15). Thus, in addition to the problem of interpretation just discussed, the Pearson procedure may not be applicable to many sets of data. In the deterrence data on imprisonment (Logan, 1972), for example, V ranges from 0.94 to 1.86.

When Pearson's formula provides a poor approximation, Chayes (1971) suggests substituting a simulation technique as an alternative means of determining a null value for the correlation of two ratios formed from three uncorrelated components. However, since Chayes' simulation technique is directly analoguous to the Pearsonian null comparison, the criticisms already made of that comparison also will apply to the simulation technique when it is being used as a substitute for Pearson's null comparison.

Still, there is another way of interpreting a simulation technique, in terms of measurement error, that seems at least intuitively compelling. What Chayes did was to generate, for a large number of simulated "cases," quasi-random values for each of three components in such a way as to reproduce the means, standard deviations, and coefficients of variation that these components have in some empirical sample data. It would seem best, however, to reproduce not only the means and standard deviations of the empirical data, as Chayes does, but the ranges as well, particularly with data that cannot take on negative values above or below a certain range because of some practical or theoretical limits.[1] With all these restrictions on the random generation, it is as if we took the actual empirical data and scrambled the values among the cases, thereby creating massive measurement error. For example, our new "case" representing Alabama might be randomly assigned California's number of prison admissions (A), Ohio's number of crimes (C), and Nevada's population size (P). These components would be random with respect to each other and the resulting ratios (A/C;C/P) would be meaningless.

Thus, if it could be shown that an empirical correlation found between theoretically meaningful ratios formed from real-data components is about the same as that which is found between theoretically meaningless ratios formed by scrambling the component data, this would certainly raise troublesome questions about the nature of the empirical correlation, even if it could not be said to definitely prove that the empirical correlation is spurious or artifactual.

A scrambled-data simulation technique. Using computer programs for random number generation and a FORTRAN sorting procedure,[2] the real values for admissions to prison (A), crimes (C), and population size (P) for 48 states were scrambled in a random fashion and then recombined into ratios A/C and C/P. These scrambled-data ratios were then correlated and their scatterplots examined. As was the case with the original (unscrambled) data, A/C and C/P correlated negatively, at moderate strength, for all felony categories. However, examination of the scatterplots showed that for every felony category a few extreme outliers gave the data a strong curve, asymptotic on both axes. This curve was present in the original data, but became more pronounced with the scrambling and recombining procedure. To adjust for the skewed distributions of A/C and C/P, and the curvilinearity of their correlation, log transformations were made on each ratio, both in the original data and in the scrambled data.

The program written to randomly scramble the values of A, C, and P, recombine them into A/C and C/P, and correlate these scrambled ratios was looped 1000 times. This produced a sampling distribution of the correlations that would obtain between A/C and C/P in a hypothetical population where A, C, and P were distributed as they are in the real world but without any correlation to each other. Since in the scrambled data A, C, and P were not related and the resultant ratios A/C and C/P had no substantive meaning or causal relation to each other,[3] the sampling distribution of scrambled-data correlations represents correlations due entirely to the artifactual effect of having a term common to both ratios. This sampling distribution can thus be used to test whether the empirical correlations found in the original data are significantly different from the average correlations that occur artifactually in the corresponding sets of scrambled data. Table 1 presents the results of this test.

Only for sex offenses is the original (real-data) correlation significantly greater than what occurs under the conditions of the scrambled-data simulation. For most felonies, the scrambled-data correlations are as high or higher than those in the original data. This does not prove that the real-data correlations are artifactual, but it does at least shake our faith in the results of published deterrence research to

Table 1: Original vs Scrambled Data Correlations Between Certainty of Imprisonment (A/C) and Crime Rate (C/P) (Log Transformed)

| | Scrambled-Data Correlations | | | |
	Mean	Standard Deviation	Original-data Correlation	p-value
Offense				
Total Felonies	-.55	.08	-.47	.37
Homicide	-.57	.08	-.19	<.001
Sex Offenses	-.60	.07	-.76	.02
Robbery	-.62	.07	-.67	.44
Assault	-.69	.05	-.71	.76
Burglary	-.54	.08	-.45	.32
Larceny	-.45	.10	-.26	.04
Auto Theft	-.38	.11	-.31	.52

NOTE: Probability of obtaining a scrambled-data correlation as far from the mean of the scrambled-data correlations as is the original-data correlation.

think that they could be replicated using data so randomly scrambled as to be meaningless. This is more remarkable than a roomful of monkeys pounding eternally on typewriters and eventually reproducing a work of Shakespeare. This is like 1,000 monkeys shredding and recomposing a data set and each one tending, on the average, to reproduce the findings of the original researcher.

In any case, this simulation experiment is sufficient to raise serious questions about the reality of at least some of the original ratio correlations that have been published in deterrence research. However, though simulation tests may demonstrate a very real possibility of spuriousness in the correlation of deterrence ratios, they do not prove its existence.

Decomposition into Component Covariances

In other treatments of problems in ratio correlation (Schuessler, 1973, 1974; Fuguitt and Lieberson, 1974), it has been observed that even when our main concern is with the correlation of ratios as ratios it may be interesting or instructive to decompose the correlation of two ratios by expressing it in terms of the covariances among the components. Schuessler (1974: 379), however, is reluctant to lay down specific guidelines as to when this should be done or the interpretations that should be placed on the various possible results, because he quite correctly recognizes that the substantive nature of the problem will determine the appropriateness and meaningfulness of this approach. This point is crucial, and will be returned to after a brief discussion of Schuessler's general approach.

Schuessler calls attention to the point that the relation between two ratios can be expressed as a function of the relation among the components with exact rather than approximate results if the variables are first converted by log transformations. Schuessler (1973: 217) notes that with log transformations the covariance of log transformed ratios can be expressed as a direct function of sums and differences of component covariances and the common term variance.

For purposes of illustration, Schuessler (1973: 217-219) took data on imprisonment and offense rates (for all Index Felonies combined) for 1966 and analyzed them by this decomposition technique. The results were:

$-.03 = (.24 + .22) - (.28 + 21)$, where

$-.03$ = the covariance of log (A/C) and log (C/P),

.24 = the covariance of A and C (logged and standardized),

.22 = the covariance of C and P (logged and standardized),

.28 = the variance of C (logged and standardized), and

.21 = the covariance of A and P (logged and standardized).

Schuessler (1973: 219) remarks that this finding "reflects the weight of the common term variance (.28) relative to the approximately equal covariances. An implication is that a positive relation between the admission rate and the crime rate is unlikely in the absence of a weak relation between the numbers of admissions and the population. Such a relation could occur, but it is not very probable."

A couple of observations are pertinent here. First, although it is not likely that the AP relation would ever be very weak in absolute terms, we may expect it to tend to be weaker than the AC or CP relations. This is because the AC and CP relations would each seem to be more direct and proximate than the AP relation. If so, then a positive ratio covariance could be expected to occur whenever the variability in crime volume is less than either the covariance between admissions and crimes or the covariance between crimes and population. Since neither of those possibilities can be rejected theoretically, it should not be concluded a priori that the ratio correlation is constrained to be negative.

Second, it should be noted that Schuessler's conclusion that the negative covariance of the ratios reflects the relative weight of the common term variance and the component covariances could just as easily be stated the other way around. It depends on what is taken as given. (Should we say that $2 + 2 = 4$ or that $4 - 2 = 2$?) The reversibility or symmetricality of the decomposition procedure is noted by Schuessler in his introduction (1973: 203), where he indicates that it may be "instructive to analyze ratio variables in terms of their components, and vice versa" (emphasis added), and again in his concluding discussion (p. 226) where he emphasizes that "the decomposition of moments of ratios into moments of components does not carry the implication that components are the causes of ratios, or vice versa." However, this point deserves even more emphasis than Schuessler gives it, because anything less than a rigorous reading of the literature on ratio correlations leaves the strong impression that expressing a correlation between ratios in terms of the moments of the components is the same as showing that the former is "due to" the latter, which is not necessarily the case.

With regard to the question of a possible artifactuality in the correlation of the deterrence variables A/C and C/P, it is not enough to be able to express the covariance of these ratios (after log transformations) in terms of moments of components, or vice versa. We still want to know what would be the correlation of A/C and C/P if it were not for the statistical effect of the common term—i.e., if the effect of that common term could somehow be removed or adjusted for. This adjustment can be accomplished through partialling, or residualizing, procedures.

Part Correlation and Use of Residual Scores

One solution to the common-term problem that has been suggested in the deterrence literature (Logan, 1972) is the use of part correlation. The general formula for part correlation is:

$$r_{1(2.3)} = \frac{r_{12} - r_{13}r_{23}}{\sqrt{1 - r_{23}^2}} , \qquad [3]$$

which expresses the correlation between 1 and the residuals of 2 regressed on 3 (Dubois, 1957: 60-62; McNemar, 1969: 186). Its significance can be tested by the formula:

$$F = \frac{r_{1(2.3)}^2}{\left(1 - R_{1.23}^2\right) / (N-3)} , \qquad [4]$$

where $R_{1.23}^2$ is the multiple correlation of 1 with 2 and 3 (McNemar, 1969: 322). The choice between part and partial correlation may be arbitrary, or it may in some cases be guided by theoretical considerations in the specification of the model.

In terms of the present, the part correlation $r_{C/P(A/C.1/C)}$ expresses the correlation of crime rate with certainty of punishment after the effects of the common term, C, have been removed from the certainty measure. $1/C$ is used here instead of C in order to meet the linearity assumption. A/C is a curvilinear function of C, but a linear function of $1/C$ (Fleiss and Tanur, 1971: 44).

Fuguitt and Lieberson (1974: 140) express reservations about the part correlation technique and conclude that "until more work is done on the rationale for part or partial correlations to remove the effect of a common term we prefer the straightforward Pearson procedure." Citing Fleiss and Tanur (1971), they point out that it can be shown for the special case of data generated such that A, C, and P are unrelated, the value of

$$r_{\frac{A}{C}\ \frac{C}{P}} \cdot C$$

and of

$$r_{\frac{A}{C}\ \frac{C}{P}} \cdot \frac{1}{C}$$

will be 0. Hence, for these data the part correlation

$$r_{\frac{C}{P}}\left(\frac{A}{C} \cdot \frac{1}{C}\right)$$

will also $= 0$, thus providing a rationale for the use of the part correlation technique *"but under the assumption that [A, C, and P] are independent. Hence it is not clear that Logan has circumvented the objection that an independence assumption is unreasonable"* (emphasis added).

However, this confuses the conditions under which a technique is proven to work, with the conditions under which the technique may be applied. Fleiss and Tanur created random data in order to demonstrate that a partial correlation would be zero when applied to data where it was known that it should be zero. Unlike the Pearson pro-

Table 2: Zero-Order vs Part Correlations Between Certainty of Imprisonment (A/C) and Crime Rate (C/P), Using Original and Scrambled Data Values (Log Transformed)

| | Original Data | | 1000 Scrambled-Data Part Correlations | |
	$r_{\frac{A}{C}\frac{C}{P}}$	$r_{\frac{C}{P}}$ (A/C.1/C)	Mean	Standard Deviation
Offense				
Total Felonies	-.47	-.30	..00	.09
Homicide	-.19	-.11	.00	.09
Sex Offenses	-.76	-.22	.00	.10
Robbery	-.67	-.20	.00	.08
Assault	-.71	-.13	.00	.08
Burglary	-.45	-.12	.00	.10
Larceny	-.26	-.14	.00	.10
Auto Theft	-.31	-.22	.00	.10

cedure, however, the application of the part correlation to real data does not *require* that we assume, even provisionally for purpose of test, that the ratio components are uncorrelated. Its advantage is that it can be applied to data where the components are known to be correlated.

The rationale for the use of part or partial correlation in the analysis of ratio variables is the same as the rationale for any use of part of partial correlation. No difference is made by the fact that in ordinary partialling analyses the controlled "third variable" is thought to be *causally* antecedent to or intervening between the other two variables, whereas in the present problem, the common term is thought to be definitionally or analytically related to the ratio variables of interest, as well as perhaps causally prior to one of them (A/C).

Thus, it would seem that part correlation ought to provide a sensible answer to the question of how A/C and C/P would correlate in the absence of any effect of the common term. In Table 2, columns 1 and 2 compare the zero-order and part correlations as calculated from the original imprisonment data. When adjustments are made for the effects of the common term, the correlations reduce considerably but do not vanish completely.

Columns 3 and 4 of Table 2 illustrate the application of part correlation to the scrambled data, where the values of A/C, C/P, and 1/C are known to be meaningless and unrelated except for the effect of the common term. As expected, the part correlations for those data reduce to an average value of zero, though they may depart from zero by chance in any one trial.

In comparing column 2 with columns 3 and 4, it can be seen that several of the original-data part correlations are low enough that their reliability or reality might be questioned. The values for homicide, burglary, assault, and larceny are that low, while the values for total felonies, sex offenses, auto theft, and robbery remain high enough to have confidence in their reliability or reality.

In sum, then, the application of part correlation techniques to these data suggests that for all eight offense categories, the common term may be acting as an artificial inflator of the correlations between sanction rates and crime rates. For about half the felony categories there may even be no nonchance correlation once the common term is removed. [4]

Part correlation provides a method of testing for the existence and degree of artifactual common-term effects in a simple two-variable analysis. An extension of part correlation to the multivariate case would be to regress one ratio on the common term, creating a new variable out of the residual score. This score would then be used in all further analyses as a measure of the first variable that should have no definitional contamination with the second variable.

Additional variables could then be entered into the analysis using standard multivariate techniques.

CONCLUSION

Some definite limitations must be admitted in drawing conclusions from this chapter. First, the methodological arguments were not proofs, in any rigorous sense. Rather, they were largely intuitive, logical, or—in the use of the scrambled and simulated data—empirical. Second, the applications to actual deterrence data have been limited to one particular data set. This data set, however, is one that has been analyzed independently by several researchers and is very similar to data used by most others who have examined the deterrent effects of imprisonment and may therefore be taken as representative of a considerable portion of the data analyzed in cross-sectional deterrence research.

Keeping these limitations in mind, two general conclusions—one substantive and one methodological—may be hazarded.

The substantive conclusion is that confident assertions that deterrence "works" (cf. Tullock, 1974) are premature. It has not been shown that current variations in imprisonment rates have a causal influence on crime rates, whether through deterrence or simple incapacitation. Indeed, while much attention has been paid to such problems as causal order and control of antecedent variables in interpreting the correlations found, too little attention may have been paid to the logically primary question of the possible artifactuality of those correlations in the first place. The questions raised in this chapter ought to at least encourage some more systematic examination of the issue of possible artifactuality in the findings of much recent and current deterrence research.

The general methodological conclusion is that the most useful test for the existence of a common-term artifact in a bivariate ratio correlation is the technique of part correlation. Where additional variables are included, the best approach would seem to be to residualize one of the two ratio variables by regressing it on the common term and proceed from there.

NOTES

1. Previous attempts in the deterrence literature to use simulation techniques to investigate the possibility of a common-term artifact have either failed to set any limits at all on the simulated data (Tittle, 1969) or constrained the simulated components only by the ranges of the real data (Chiricos and Waldo, 1970; Logan, 1971).

2. Details of this scrambling procedure can be made available on request.

3. The truth of this was verified empirically with the scrambled data.

4. This is in contrast to earlier conclusions based on part correlations (Logan, 1972), where the effect of log transformations on part correlations were not considered, nor were comparisons made with the application of part correlation to scrambled data.

REFERENCES

American Friends Service Committee (1971) Struggle for Justice. New York: Hill & Wang.

ANTUNES, G. and A. L. HUNT (1973) "The impact of certainty and severity of punishment on levels of crime in American states: an extended analysis." J. of Criminal Law, Criminology and Police Sci. 64 (December): 486-493.

BAILEY, W. C., D. J. MARTIN, and L. N. GRAY (1971) "Crime and deterrence: a correlation analysis." (mimeo)

BEAN, F. and R. CUSHING (1971) "Criminal homicide, punishment and deterrence: methodological and substantive reconsiderations." Social Sci. Q. 52 (September): 277-289.

BLOCK, M. K. (1972) "An economic analysis of theft with special emphasis on household decisions under uncertainty." Ph.D. dissertation, Stanford University.

CHAPMAN, J. I. (1973) "The impact of police on crime and crime on police: a synthesis of the economic and ecological approaches." Institute of Government and Public Affairs, UCLA. (mimeo)

CHAYES, F. (1971) Ratio Correlation: A Manual for Students of Petrology and Geochemistry. Chicago: Univ. of Chicago Press.

CHIRICOS, T. G. and G. P. WALDO (1970) "Punishment and crime: an examination of some empirical evidence." Social Problems 18 (Fall): 200-217.

DUBOIS, P. H. (1957) Multivariate Correctional Analysis. New York: Harper & Row.

EHRLICH, I. (1975) "The deterrent effect of capital punishment: a question of life and death." Amer. Economic Rev. 65 (June): 397-417.

——— (1973) "Participation in illegitimate activities: a theoretical and empirical investigation." J. of Pol. Economy 81 (May): 521-565.

——— (1972) "The deterrent effect of criminal law enforcement." J. of Legal Studies 1 (June): 259-276.

ERICKSON, M. and J. GIBBS (1973) "The deterrence question: some alternative methods of analysis." Social Sci. Q. 54 (December): 534-551.

FLEISS, J. L. and J. M. Tanur (1971) "A note on the partial correlation coefficient." Amer. Statistian 25 (February): 42-45.

FREEMAN, J. H. and J. E. KRONENFELD (1973) "Problems of definitional dependency: the case of administrative intensity." Social Forces 52 (September): 108-121.

FUGUITT, G. V. and S. LIEBERSON (1974) "Correlation of ratios or difference scores having common terms," pp. 128-144 in H. L. Costner (ed.) Sociological Methodology 1973-1974.

GIBBS, J. P. (1968) "Crime, punishment and deterrence." Southwestern Social Sci. Q. 48 (March): 515-530.

GRAY, L. and D. J. MARTIN (1969) "Punishment and deterrence: another analysis of Gibbs' data." Social Sci. Q. 50 (September): 389-395.

KOBRIN, S., S. G. LUBECK, E. W. HANSEN, and R. YEAMAN (1973) The Deterrent Effectiveness of Criminal Justice Sanction Strategies: Summary Report. Washington, DC: Law Enforcement Assistance Administration, National Institute of Law Enforcement and Criminal Justice.

KUH, E. and J. R. MEYER (1955) "Correlations and regression estimates when data are ratios." Econometrica 23 (January): 400-416.

LOGAN, C. H. (1975) "Arrest rates and deterrence." Social Sci. Q. 56 (December): 376-389.

——— (1972) "General deterrent effects of imprisonment." Social Forces 51 (September): 64-73.

——— (1971) "On punishment and crime (Chiricos and Waldo, 1970): some methodological commentary." Social Problems 19 (Winter): 280-284.

McNEMAR, Q. (1969) Psychological Statistics. New York: John Wiley.

MORRIS, N. (1974) The Future of Imprisonment. Chicago: Univ. of Chicago Press.

PEARSON, K. (1897) "Mathematical contributions to the theory of evolution: on a form of spurious correlation which may arise when indices are used in the measurement of organs." Proceedings of the Royal Society of London 60: 489-498.

PHILLIPS, L. and H. VOTEY, Jr. (1972) "An economic analysis of the deterrent effect of law enforcement on criminal activities." J. of Criminal Law, Criminology, and Police Sci. 63 (September): 336-342.

RANGARAJAN, C. and S. CHATTERJEE (1969) "A note on comparison between correlation coefficients of original and transformed variables." Amer. Statistician 23 (October): 28-29.

SCHUESSLER, K. (1974) "Analysis of ratio variables: opportunities and pitfalls." Amer. J. of Sociology 80 (September): 379-396.

——— (1973) "Ratio variables and path models," pp. 201-228 in A. S. Goldberger and O. D. Duncan (eds.) Structural Equation Models in the Social Sciences. New York: Seminar Press.

——— (1952) "The deterrent influence of the death penalty." Annals of the American Academy of Political and Social Science 284: 54-62.

TITTLE C. R. (1969) "Crime rates and legal sanctions." Social Problems 16 (Spring): 409-423.

——— and A. R. ROWE (1974) "Certainty of arrest and crime rates: a further test of the deterrence hypothesis." Social Forces 52 (June) 455-462.

TULLOCK, G. (1974) "Does punishment deter crime?" Public Interest 36 (Summer): 103-111.

VAN DEN HAAG, E. (1975) On Punishing Criminals. Concerning an Old and Very Painful Question. New York: Basic Books.

VANDAELE, W. (1976) "Participation in illegitimate activities: I. Ehrlich revisited." Harvard University. (unpublished)

VON HIRSCH, A. (1976) Doing Justice: The Choice of Punishments. New York: Hill & Wang.

WILSON, J. Q. (1975) Thinking About Crime. New York: Basic Books.

YULE, G. U. (1910) "On the interpretation of correlations between indices or ratios." J. of the Royal Statistical Society 73: 644-647.

——— and M. G. KENDALL (1950) An Introduction to the Theory of Statistics. New York: Hafner.

Larry Cohen
*University of Illinois
at Chicago Circle*

5

SANCTION THREATS AND VIOLATION BEHAVIOR:
An Inquiry into Perceptual Variation

Policy makers seeking guidance or support for their crime control efforts will find little assistance in the current deterrence literature. A decade of intense empirical inquiry has produced conflicting evidence on the relationship between sanctions and law-regarding behavior. These results suggest that deterrence should not be treated as a universal phenomenon, but rather as one whose effects are dependent on conditions related to the situation, the individual, or some combination of both of them (Erikson and Gibbs, 1973). This seems a reasonable interpretation in view of the "internal" nature of the deterrence process: specifically, that deterrent effects depend on the individual's perception, first of the possibility and then of the consequences of detection, apprehension, and punishment. Since perceptions can be expected to vary across situations and among individuals, the efficacy of sanction threats should vary as well. Students of deterrence would then be pressed to explore and explain these variations if they expect to account for the contingent quality of deterrent effects and, ultimately, to provide an adequate theory

AUTHOR'S NOTE: Invaluable comments and suggestions by Eric Moskowitz and George Balch are gratefully acknowledged.

of general deterrence. This study is a preliminary effort toward those ends.

When defined as a problem of perception, the contingency question is most profitably approached, as here, through an "individual" level analysis. Ecological data can provide useful insights, but because varying individual perceptions and behavior are aggregated, the results are necessarily ambiguous with respect to the extent of and reasons for these variations. Individual data is no panacea, but it does permit a more direct examination of the socio-psychological correlates of these perceptions, and also consideration of what for policy makers is surely a most important question, the susceptibility of perceptions to change.

The research reported below focused on the perceptions and behavior of motor vehicle operators relative to speed control laws. The threat references in this case are the probability of receiving a citation for speeding in a given jurisdiction and the degree of punishment associated with that citation. Given a distribution of values assigned to these threats by the motorists, it was possible to examine whether these perceptions change as individuals cross jurisdictional boundaries, and then whether differences in perception can account for differences in the level of speeding behavior. Finally, the analysis considered whether the perceptual variation observed for the base jurisdiction can be explained by (1) peer association, (2) the nature of one's experience as a law violator, or (3) such personal characteristics as age, income, and education. Before proceeding to the analysis and results it may be helpful to briefly review previous research bearing on these several explanatory factors.

EXPLAINING SANCTION PERCEPTIONS

This discussion assumes that deterrence can be viewed as a communication process. Sanction messages are transmitted by police and adjudicative agencies and are received and interpreted by members of the target population. In this context, perceptual variation is the result of distortion engendered either by the transmission of an ambiguous message or by factors in the communication process which systematically filter or modify the content of the message. The problem of ambiguity will be addressed later in the context of observed differences in the subjects' knowledge of the certainty and severity of punishment. The filtering factors discussed below are not necessarily the primary causes of distortion, but surely are among those which a more complete examination of distortion must consider.

Peer Association

Certainly one explanation for differences in perception is the type of group with whom one associates. There is considerable evidence that individual's beliefs tend to be consonant with those of the collective. The classic example of this group influence is the small group judgment-conflict experiment. A single adult gives the obviously correct judgment in a situation and is then confronted with the unanimous, but obviously incorrect judgment of other members of the group. Under such conditions there is a significant tendency for the single adult to shift from a correct to an incorrect position (Asch, 1951). Becker (1963) described a similarly influential process in the development and perpetuation of beliefs among members of deviant groups. Finally, a recent study of marijuana smokers noted a much lower expectation of apprehension if one's friends were also users than if they were not. The study concluded that "drug using groups provide the context for release from conventional controls and supports for use through articulation of beliefs and attitudes which discount both the fear of apprehension and arguments relating to the negative aspects of use" (Burkett and Jensen, 1975: 530). When distinctive groups articulate sets of beliefs about sanction threats we should find similar systematic differences in their respective perceptions of the sanction threat.

Experience as a Law Violator

As with any learning process it seems reasonable to expect that the more one successfully engages in law-violating behavior, the more confident one becomes of his or her own ability to act without detection. Several studies observed that law violators were more likely to believe that they could avoid apprehension and punishment than were law-abiders (Claster, 1967; Jensen, 1969; Kraut, 1976), although one study found that this relationship depended on the kind of offense involved (Chirocos and Waldo, 1972). This analysis is concerned with the same general issue, but necessarily approaches it in a different way. The avoider/offender distinction is not viable with speeding offenses because, as we shall see, the vast majority of motorists admit to some speeding behavior. A more appropriate question, then, is whether successful violators differ in their perceptions from unsuccessful ones.

Learning theory again suggests a reasonable hypothesis: successful violators will have been reinforced in their beliefs that they can avoid the sanction and thus tend to perceive a less certain and less severe punishment than will those who have been sanctioned. Deterrence theory, where it focuses on those already punished ("special deterrence"), similarly expects that the "experience of punishment would tend to strengthen fear" (Andenaes, 1974: 176). These predictions assume, of course, that the sanctioning process is in fact more certain and more severe than those unexperienced believe it to be. Otherwise, "fear" will actually be lessened and deterrence processes less efficacious for those sanctioned than those not (Geerken and Gove, 1975).

Personal Characteristics

Age, income, and education level are frequently treated as surrogates for more abstract attitudes and belief systems, although there is considerable disagreement about the nature and validity of these linkages (Rosenberg, 1968). Several possible implications for perceptions of sanction threats may be suggested. For example, all three attributes might be viewed as surrogates for "system support," on the assumption that older, better educated, and wealthier people have a greater stake in the prevailing institutions and in the social and legal norms which support them. On this account, such individuals should tend to perceive a greater sanction threat than younger, less educated, and lower income people. However, one might argue that those possessing the former characteristics will feel less vulnerable to the threat because of the additional knowledge they possess about and the resources they can bring to bear in dealing with the "system." People who believe they possess such "social influence" should tend to perceive a relatively lower threat than those who do not. Other hypotheses could be offered, but the measures necessary to distinguish among them are not available here. It may therefore be more appropriate to offer the findings on these characteristics as descriptive generalizations and to defer further explication of their theoretical significance, if any, to further research.

METHOD

Subjects

A 54-item questionnaire was administered to 105 male residents of a military installation in the southwestern United States. Respondents were selected through a cluster sampling procedure that focused on installation family housing blocks. Individual households were randomly selected within blocks, with no response at 25% of those contacted and a 5% refusal rate. Subjects were told that the research was being conducted as part of an education project. Those who asked were further informed that the study had been approved by the Department of the Air Force and by the installation commander. All respondents were assured that the information they provided would remain strictly confidential.

The military environment was chosen because it provided a clearly bounded referent for police and adjudicative activities. It was thus possible to rule out potential confusion over objective threat sources. The military setting was furthermore essential for the comparative analysis, which required at least two distinct points in space. In this case the threat projected by the military agencies could be compared with that of the civilian agencies immediately outside the base. Of course, the latter is not as well bounded as the former, but the differences between the two, and especially their respective loci of responsibility, are sharp and evident. Respondents reported that most installation residents, themselves included, leave the base by car regularly, and thus could be expected to have some familiarity with both jurisdictions. Even if it cannot be assumed that the respondents were equally knowledgeable about and experienced with the traffic laws, enforcement policies, and practices in each of them, we may nonetheless examine the distinctions they make in their perceptions and behavior.

Measures

Indicators for the various perceptions and behaviors were based on questionnaire items. Those dealing with certainty and severity focused on the police and those with severity on the appropriate adjudicative mechanisms. Respondents provided both objective estimates and subjective evaluations of the threat posed by the military agencies, with this information subsequently used to locate individuals on the certainty and severity perception scales.[1] Note that this method accounts not only for the subjects' knowledge of the sanction policies, but also for beliefs about their own susceptibility to apprehension and the harshness of the penalty threatened. Separate items asked respondents to compare the likelihood of their being caught for speeding on base with their chances of being caught on the adjacent civilian roads, and to similarly compare the severity of the penalty in the two jurisdictions. Finally, self-report data on violations were used to distinguish relative levels of speeding on the installation, as reflected in a three-point scale, and also to compare speeding behavior on and off the base.

The peer influence measure focused on two large, but still distinguishable groups, the officer and the enlisted ranks. Both formal military regulations and powerful social norms maintain the independence of and distance between these ranks. While significant within-group differences are undoubtedly present and bear future consideration, this analysis assumes that a between-group comparison is viable because of the fundamentally different beliefs each maintains, especially as to power and status in the society. These differences are reinforced by the tendency to limit social interactions to others in the same group. Of course, the shared beliefs must be related to a specific issue if perceptions are to be effected. Therefore, only members of the two groups who report regularly conversing with family and friends about traffic regulations and motor vehicle operations will be included in this portion of the analysis.

Finally, citation issuance data were collected from official military police records. These records detail all traffic citations issued to the individual, as well as the penalty assessed for the violation. The data were used, among other things, to determine which of the self-admitted speeders were and were not successful in avoiding detection.

ANALYSIS AND DISCUSSION

It is evident from Table 1 that sample members did differ in their perceptions of the sanction threat associated with speeding regulations. These differences served as the focal point for the statistical analysis, which is summarized in Table 2 and discussed below. First, though, some comments are in order about the relationship between these perceptions and the threat ostensibly posed by the sanctioning mechanisms. Because the perception scales contain a subjective element they cannot be directly compared with the content of the threat messages. However, we can compare this content with a comparable objective estimate provided by the respondents.

Knowledge of Sanction Practices

Of note is the respondents' inaccurate information

Table 1: Variation in Perception

SINGLE (MILITARY) JURISDICTION PERCEPTIONS

Certainty of Apprehension (N=105)		Severity of Punishment (N=105)	
Low Probability	24.8%	Weak Penalty	34.4%
Moderate Probability	40.0%	Moderate Penalty	48.8%
High Probability	35.2%	Severe Penalty	16.8%

ACROSS (MILITARY VS. CIVILIAN) JURISDICTION PERCEPTIONS

Certainty Compared (N=99)		Severity Compared (N=99)	
Lower Probability-Civilian	8.1%	Weaker Penalty-Civilian	26.3%
About Same Probability	22.2%	About Same Penalty	15.1%
Higher Probability-Civilian	69.7%	More Severe Penalty-Civilian	58.6%

about enforcement policies on the one hand and generally accurate information about punishment policies on the other. During the three months preceding the interviews, an average 3.2 citations were issued each day for speeding (Sd = 3.0) and 4.2 for all traffic offenses combined (Sd = 3.6). Of the respondents, 98% predicted higher amounts, with a modal estimate of 10 (17%), a mean of 39.6 (Sd = 127.3), and 7% estimated more than 65 citations per day. In using "citations issued" as an indicator of the probability of apprehension it is necessary to assume that the number of offenses in constant over time (e.g., $P = C/O = C \cdot K$, where P is the probability of apprehension, C the number of citations issued, O the total number of speeding violations, and K is a constant). The assumption is admittedly problematic, but unavoidable in view of the absence of police records regarding the level of violation behavior.

Respondents were much better informed about the penalty assessed for speeding violations. Military policy limits this penalty to one from a hierarchy ranging from verbal counseling to written counseling, written reprimands, and license suspension. Police records revealed that in nearly all cases (90%) the lowest punishment was

Table 2: Summary of Findings

PERCEIVED SANCTION THREATS AND VIOLATION BEHAVIOR

Single (Military) Jurisdiction

	Perceived Certainty	Perceived Severity
Speeding Behavior	$-.37^d$	.03
	$(-.34)$	$(.02)$

Across (Military vs. Civilian) Jurisdictions

	Perceived Certainty	Perceived Severity
Speeding Behavior	$-.16^b$	.02
	$(-.19)$	$(.02)$

EXPLAINING PERCEPTUAL VARIATION

	Experience as Violator	Peer Association	Age	Education	Income
Perceived Certainty	$-.10$	$-.12$	.11	$-.17^b$	$-.09$
	$(-.02)$	$(-.11)$	$(.14)$	$(-.10)$	$(-.09)$
Perceived Severity	$-.25^c$	$.22^c$	.05	$-.15^b$	.10
	$(-.20)$	$(.18)$	$(.02)$	$(-.11)$	$(.02)$

a. Parametric statistics (Pearson product moment coefficients) were used in the analysis reported in the text, because they were required for the multivariate analyses. Since the indicators are mostly ordinal, though, a nonparametric statistic (Kendall's Tau, in parentheses) is reported here as well.
b. p   .05
c. p   .01
d. p   .001

used. Of the respondents, 32% correctly identified verbal counseling as the punishment they expected to receive; 12% mentioned fines and license suspension. The rest expected to have points assessed on their traffic records, and of these, 50% (or 28% of the total) identified the correct number of points in a hypothetical situation. Technically, point assessment is not a valid response, since military regulations explicitly treat it as an administrative and not a punitive measure. Still, respondents might reasonably view it as punitive since an accumulation of a large number of points over a short period of time would result in revocation of on-base driving privileges.

These differences in knowledge can be related to the varying levels of ambiguity in the respective threat messages. Both messages necessarily suffer some ambiguity because of the discretion available to police and commanders. Still, there are some concrete referents for the penalty imposed, first in the military regulations and second in public statements about the policies actually followed. These provide substance to the severity message which individuals can draw upon when speculating about and discussing the punishment they may receive. There is no comparable substance in the message relating to the probability of apprehension. Police policies are not normally publicized, and even where they are their significance cannot be precisely determined. This leaves the value of the threat open to conjecture, resulting in the substantial variance observed here on one estimate relating to these practices. This has the disadvantage of leaving open the possibility that the threat of apprehension will be consistently underestimated and perhaps ignored. However, it may just as well serve the interests of the police where, as here, the tendency is to overestimate the threat (Jensen, 1969). As we will note later, these differences in the ambiguity of the messages have important implications for efforts to enhance the efficacy of deterrent sanctions.

Perceived Threats and Violation Behavior-On Base

The findings are essentially consistent with those of previous research (Anderson et al., 1977). First, there is a moderate, inverse relationship between perceived certainty and speeding behavior ($r = .37$; $p < .001$), but no relationship between perceived severity and behavior ($r = .03$). Together, these two dimensions of the sanction threat account for 13.3% of the variance, but most of this is due to the certainty factor (13.1%). Scatterplots do not reveal any further noteworthy relationships between the variables.

Continuing reports of support for certainty but not severity lend weight to the argument that the level of punishment is not a viable aspect of the deterrent threat. However, one reasonable counterclaim is that severity matters, but only when persons believe there is a high probability that they will receive that punishment. The underlying logic is simple, obvious, and central to the notion of deterrence, yet it has received little systematic attention (Erikson and Gibbs, 1973). This hypothesis was explored here by constructing an interaction term composed of the two sanction dimensions and then examining its independent contribution to the explained variance in speeding behavior. It adds virtually nothing to that already accounted for by certainty alone, suggesting that, at least with this data set, severity is not modified by certainty.

Another possible counterclaim focuses on the allegedly "trivial" punishment involved. The motorist may be troubled by the inconvenience of being stopped for speeding and by the social stigma associated with receiving a citation, but feel little additional concern about being counseled or assessed a few points (unless the cumulative total places him near or over the revocation level). Perhaps if the usual penalty for speeding had been used, e.g., a small fine, then motorists might be more responsive to the punitive aspect of the deterrent threat. This can be examined by noting changes in perception and reported behavior when a jurisdication which imposes a small fine is considered.

Perceived Threats and Violation
Behavior—Across Jurisdictions

Significantly, individuals did perceive differences in the threats posed by different legal environments (Table 1), and furthermore reported adjusting their speeding behavior when they left the installation: 57.8% indicated that they speed more and 6.6% that they speed less on civilian than on military roads. Yet virtually none of this change in behavior is explained by changes in perception of the sanction threat. While there is a weak, independent relationship between behavior and perceived certainty ($r = -.16$; $p < .05$), there is no relationship whatever with perceived severity.

Scatterplots are again not particularly helpful in evaluating the findings, except that they do highlight two interesting clusters of responses: 51% of the respondents reported, as expected, that they speed more on civilian roads, which they believe are in a lower certainty environment; however, 37% indicated that the civilian jurisdiction had a more severe punishment policy, but nonetheless reported speeding *more* there than on the installation. Perhaps the latter individuals regard the certainty threat off base to be so low that they feel they can ignore an even more severe penalty, although this implies an interaction effect which we have already discounted. Alternately, one might argue that the threat of a small fine is still too weak to influence behavior and that a much harsher penalty must be imposed for severity to be effective. This latter claim bears further consideration, although it should be noted that most jurisdictions consider a small fine to be the just penalty for all but frequently identified speeders and that efforts to impose much harsher measures have found them difficult to maintain over time (Campbell and Ross, 1968).

Explaining Perceptual Variation

Taken together, the several factors examined here explained little of the variance in perceptions of certainty and severity, and left virtually unchanged the strength of the relationships between sanctions and behavior. Still, a few of the bivariate relationships were statistically significant and merit closer consideration.

First, it was suggested earlier that violators who avoided detection would perceive a less certain and less severe punishment than would those who had been cited. These expectations are modestly supported for severity ($r = -.25$; $p < .01$), but not for certainty ($r = -.10$). One possible explanation for the latter finding is that the avoidance rate for speeding is so large that a cited offender may reasonably assume that he was the victim of a random process and is not likely to be detected again, certainly no more likely than anyone else.[2] Those familiar with police enforcement practices would probably concur with this characterization (Gardiner, 1969).

The significant finding with severity should similarly be evaluated in the context of the mechanism through which it is applied. Unlike enforcement, the penalizing process is conducted in a systematic and consistent manner. Motorists experienced with that process would have learned that everyone gets essentially the same penalty for speeding. Those not cited, and hence less directly familiar with it, may believe that the penalty could be minimized or avoided in their own case and thus tend to value it less than would those who know otherwise. It may be objected that this penalty is an unusually minor one and probably less than what those unfamiliar with the process would expect. Thus, the opposite relationship between perceived severity and violation experience should obtain. Recall, however, that sample members were well informed about the basic penalty commonly applied, and there was little difference in the knowledge of cited and uncited individuals. It therefore appears that they are evaluating the same objective threat differently depending on whether or not they suffered its imposition.

Perceptual variation should also result when distinct groups support competing beliefs that bear on the sanction threat. The obvious beliefs to consider when examining military groups are those dealing with relative access to power and authority. Since officers occupy the ostensibly superior roles in this environment, they should share and, as a group, reinforce beliefs that emphasize their ability to control that environment, while enlisted men, because of their subordinate position, should tend to feel more at the mercy of processes external to themselves. If these assumptions are correct, then it can be hypothesized that officers will feel less threatened by the activities of the enforcement agency and be less fearful of the minor penalty associated with a citation than will those in the enlisted ranks. The evidence, however, reveals no relationship with perceived certainty ($r = .12$) and the opposite of what was expected with perceived severity ($r = .22$;

$p<.01$).While inconsistent with the predictions and in need of further explanation, these findings do at least partially support the claim that there is a peer association effect on perception of sanctions.

Perhaps the finding for severity can be reconciled if we take a more instrumental view of the way each of these groups evaluates the penalty. Officers do occupy potentially more powerful roles than those in the enlisted ranks, but they are in some senses more restricted in their conduct. Whereas enlisted men are evaluated almost exclusively on their job performance, officers are further judged on their general military "bearing." In this context, different norms regarding social and professional advancement may be present and result in differential evaluation of the seriousness of this minor penalty. Given this logic, though, the lack of any relationship with perceptions of certainty remain puzzling. The explanation may be that the police, who are identified with the threat of apprehension, bear no different relationship to the status concerns of officers and enlisted men, but the commanders who will mete out the penalty can be expected to judge members of the two ranks in discriminating and consequential ways.

Only one of the personal characteristics was related to the sanction perceptions. There was a weak tendency for better educated men to perceive less certain ($r = -.17$; $p < .05$) and less severe ($r = -.15$; $p < .05$) punishment than those less educated, while age and income appear to have no effect. There was furthermore no indication from the scatterplots of any nonlinear relationships between these characteristics and the threat perceptions.

CONCLUSIONS

Application of a deterrence strategy entails a concern that the disutility of a given sanction outweighs the utility of the violation behavior at issue. Yet it is evident from this and other "perception" level studies that policy makers must be further concerned with the nature of the message which conveys this sanction threat to the public. The findings reported here should of course be interpreted in the context of the specific behavior and sample population examined and of the methodological design employed. Within these constraints, though, we may conclude not only that the sanction threat is differentially perceived within the population and that these differences have apparent consequences for behavior, but also that the observed perceptual variation may be systematically related to various contextual and psychological factors. The latter conclusion is necessarily tentative in view of the scope and results of this analysis. However, if supported in future research, it should help account for the variable impact of deterrent sanctions and furthermore suggest to policy makers how deterrence messages may be more effectively communicated.

NOTES

1. Specific details on the construction of all scales used in the study is available from the author.
2. The Avoidance Rate is defined by the following equation:

$$A = (O - C)/O,$$

where A is the avoidance rate, O the total number of offenses, and C the number of citations issued.

REFERENCES

ANDENAES, J. (1974) Punishment and Deterrence. Ann Arbor: Univ. of Michigan Press.

ANDERSON, L. S., G. P. WALDO, and T. G. CHIROCOS (1977) "A longitudinal approach to the study of deterrence." Presented at the annual meeting of the American Sociological Association, Chicago.

ASCH, S. E. (1951) "Effects of group pressure upon the modification and distortion of judgments," pp. 177-191 in H. Guetzhow (ed.) Groups, Leadership and Men. Pittsburgh: Carnegie Press.

BECKER, H. (1963) Outsiders: Studies in the Sociology of Deviance. New York: Free Press.

BURKETT, S. R. and E. L. JENSEN (1975) "Conventional ties, peer influence and the fear of apprehension: a study of adolescent marijuana use." Soc. Q. 16 (Autumn): 522-533.

CAMPBELL, D. T. and H. L. ROSS (1968) "Connecticut crackdown on speeding: time series data in quasi-experimental analysis." Law and Society Rev. 3 (August): 33-76.

CASPER, J. (1972) American Criminal Justice: The Defendent's Perspective. Englewood Cliffs, NJ: Prentice-Hall.

CHIROCOS, T. and G. P. WALDO (1972) "Perceived penal sanctions and self-reported criminality: a neglected approach to deterrence research." Social Problems 19: 522-540.

CLASTER, D. (1967) "Comparisons of risk perception between delinquents and non-delinquents." J. of Criminal Law, Criminology and Police Sci. 58 (March): 80-86.

ERIKSON, M. L. and J. P. GIBBS (1973) "The deterrence doctrine: some alternative methods of analysis." Social Sci. Q. 54 (December): 534-551.

GARDINER, J. (1969) Traffic and the Police: Variations in Law Enforcement Policy. Cambridge, MA: Harvard Univ. Press.

GIBBS, J. P. (1975) Crime Punishment and Deterrence. New York: Elsevier.

GRASMICK, H. G. and L. APPLETON (1977) "Legal punishment and social stigma: a comparison of two deterrence models." Social Sci. Q. 58 (June): 15-28.

JENSEN, G. (1969) "Crime doesn't pay: correlates of a shared misunderstanding." Social Problems 17 (Fall): 189-201.

KRAUT, R. E. (1976) "Deterrence and definitional influences on shoplifting." Social Problems 23 (February): 358-368.

PLATE, T. (1975) Crime Pays! New York: Simon & Schuster.

ROSENBERG, M. (1968) The Logic of Survey Analysis. New York: Basic Books.

WALDO, G. P. and T. G. CHIROCOS (1972) "Perceived penal sanction and self-reported criminality: a neglected approach to deterrence research." Social Problems 19 (Spring): 522-540.

Gideon Vigderhous
Bell Canada

6

CYCLICAL VARIATIONS OF MONTHLY AND YEARLY HOMICIDE RATES IN THE UNITED STATES AND THEIR RELATIONSHIP TO CHANGES IN THE UNEMPLOYMENT RATE

In the criminological literature, one can find numerous accounts which describe and evaluate time series of crime rates. These studies report on percent increase of crime rates or provide a simple form of trend analysis. Another area which criminologists found of interest is the identification of seasonal fluctuations or temporal variations of crime rates. Findings from these studies are not consistent and are often contradictory. A major problem found in these studies is that they employ a "weak" methodological strategy in the analysis of time series. Cyclical variations of crime rates cannot be accurately identified by simple observation of graphical presentations or other descriptive methods.

In light of these criticisms, the purpose of this chapter is to provide a systematic statistical analysis of homicide rates in the United States based on monthly and yearly data. The monthly data cover the period 1963-1974 and the yearly data cover the period 1900-1974. Specifically, an attempt will be made to answer the following questions:

(1) what are the cyclical movements of monthly and yearly homicide rates?

(2) how can we utilize the knowledge of time series analysis or crime rates to forecast violent crimes?

The general interest in time series analysis of crime rates can take two distinctive approaches: (1) to investigate the seasonal and cyclical movements of crime rates, (2) to investigate the socioeconomic determinants of violent crimes. The two approaches could be linked by identifying leading indicators which can be utilized in building a forecasting model of crime rates. Specifically, if criminologists will be able to identify, on the macro social level, socioeconomic or demographic factors which can explain the temporal variations in crime rates, then this information could be utilized in building more effective forecasting models of crime rates.

Background

The phenomenon of violent crimes and particularly criminal homicide received wide attention from criminologists. One of the most extensive studies on homicide was conducted by Wolfgang (1958), where the different patterns of homicide were studied in Philadelphia between January 1948 and December 1952. This study provided a detailed socioeconomic and demographic characterization of offenders and victims involved in the incidence of homicide. With reference to the cyclical variations of homicide rates, Wolfgang (1958: 321) concluded that "there is no significant association either by season or by month of year." Although homicide tends to increase during the summer months, Wolfgang concluded that there are no significant cyclical variations of homicide rates. His conclusions were based on simple observations of the time series. However, without employing statistical techniques which aim to identify cyclical variations in a given time series, such conclusions are questionable. Elwin (1943) reported that there is strong association between the hot season and the frequency of homicide. (This study was conducted on the Maria tribe in India). Tardiff (1966) concluded, on the basis of Montreal data, that there is no consistent pattern variation of homicide rates and similar conclusions were reached in studies conducted in Israel, Ceylon, and Florence.[1]

Methodology

The first statistical tool utilized in analyzing yearly and monthly homicide rates is known as spectral analysis. This technique is not completely new in criminological research and was used by McPheters and Stronge (1974) in studying reported crimes of robbery, assault, burglary, larceny, and auto theft in Tampa, Florida, for the period January 1961 through December 1972. Spectral analysis is a statistical technique which can identify the cyclical components of time series. This method decomposes a stationary time series into a number of cycles. The relative contribution of each cycle to the total variance of the time series could be examined and their statistical significance could be established. A time series which is considered a random process or "white noise" will not manifest any significant cyclical movement. Spectral analysis has a long history of application in the areas of engineering, physics, and oceanography, and recently spectral analysis received wide attention from behavioral scientists, particularly from the economists Granger and Hatanaka (1964) and Fishman (1969); in marketing research from Farley and Hinich (1969), and MacKay (1973); in sociology from Mayer and Arney (1974), and more. Given a time series of homicide rates which fluctuate about a given mean, the question that arises is what is the period required for homicide to complete a specific cycle or the length of time required for the phenomenon of homicide to repeat itself? If, for example, it will take 6 months for homicide to reach its highest and lowest peaks, then the period of the homicide cycle is 6 months. Generally, cyclical variations of homicide rates can be identified by spectral analysis.

This statistical technique could be viewed as a form of regression analysis which attempts to fit sine and cosine waves into the data. (A technical discussion on spectral analysis for nonmathematicians can be found in Chan and

Hayya, 1976). Advance discussions of spectral analysis can be found in Jenkins and Watts (1968). Spectral analysis of time series is conducted on stationary time series. This concept implies that the statistical analysis should be conducted on a series with a constant mean and variance. Since crime data usually manifest a strong trend, it is essential that the trend will be removed from the data. There are several approaches to remove the trend from the series and, in this chapter, stationarity was achieved by taking the first differences of crime rates. Hence, each observation in the new series is computed from the differences between two consecutive observations of the original series - $\Delta y_t = y_t - y_{t-1}$.

Spectral analysis is analysis of time series in the frequency domain and, in conducting the analysis and reporting the results, a reference is made to the frequency of the series. The frequency refers to the number of cycles per time unit; in this study it is the number of cycles per month. If we will denote the period of homicide cycle to itself as P, then 1/P is the frequency. For example, the frequency relating to a period of 6 months is 0.1666. (The frequency varies between 0.5 to ∞.)

An important tool in spectral analysis is the autocorrelation function which is computed for different time lag — K.

$$\rho_K = \frac{\text{Cov}(Z_t, Z_{t+K})}{\sqrt{\text{Var}(Z_t)\,\text{Var}(Z_{t+K})}} \qquad [1]$$

where K = 0,1,2 . . . L.

Equation 1 includes only one variable Z_t, hence, if we consider Z_t as the homicide rate then we calculate the correlation of homicide rates for different time lags. The correlation of the time series with itself at lag K = 0 is 1.0. The

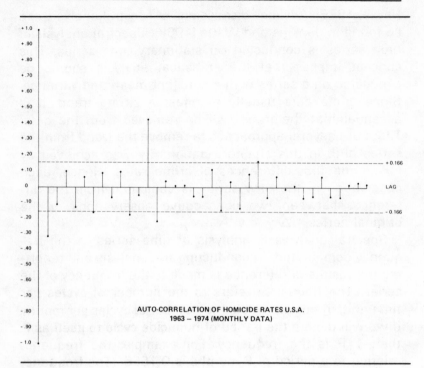

AUTO-CORRELATION OF HOMICIDE RATES U.S.A.
1963 — 1974 (MONTHLY DATA)

Figure 1

numerator of equation 1 is noted as the autocovariance function which is computed as follows:

$$\text{Cov}(K) = \frac{1}{N} \sum_{t=1}^{N-K} (Z_t - \overline{Z})(Z_{t+K} - \overline{Z}). \qquad [2]$$

However, when the series is stationary, it is expected that $\text{Var}(Z_t) = \text{Var}(Z_{t+K}) = \text{Cov}(0)$. Hence, we utilize only the auto-covariance for lag 0 in calculating the autocorrelation function. The sample autocorrelation function is presented as follows:

$$r(K) = \frac{\text{Cov}(K)}{\text{Cov}(0)}. \qquad [3]$$

The variance σ^2 of the time series is equal to the auto-covariance measure at time lag (K =0). Figure 1 represents the autocorrelation function (A.C.F.) of monthly homicide rates for the period January 1963 to December 1974.

This figure is also known as correlogram and provides most useful information on the nature of the time series. If the time series of homicide rates would constitute a random process of "white noise" then the A.C.F. values would tend to be zero with the exception of $r(0) = 1.0$. It is possible to establish confidence intervals for the A.C.F. values. The 95% confidence limits are approximated by $\pm\, 2/\sqrt{N}$ where N is the number of observations in the series. From Figure 1 it is observed that significant values were observed for time lags 1, 6, 10, 12, 13, 24, which suggests that the time series of homicide rates reflect seasonal variations which cannot be considered as a random process.

The equation for estimating the spectral density at frequency w_i is presented as follows:

$$\hat{f}(w_i) = 2\left[1.0 + 2 \sum_{K=1}^{L-1} \lambda(K)\, r(K)\, \text{Cos}\left(\frac{\pi i K}{2L}\right)\right] \qquad [4]$$

where $i = 0, 1 \ldots 2L$.

An important decision which has to be made in conducting spectral analysis is to determine a truncation point for calculating the A.C.F. values. In other words, only part of the series should be used. As a general rule of thumb, 20% to 25% of the observations are used for deciding the size of L. When L is small, then the derived estimates tend to be biased. On the other hand, if L is too large, then one could identify spurious peaks in the spectral density function. The frequencies $w_i = i/2L$ if $L = 4$ then $w_i = 0, 1/2L, 2/2L, 3/2L$ or 0, 0.125, 0.25, 0.375, and so on. The computation of w_i established in the range $0 < w_i \leqslant 1/2$. By multiplying L by 2 in equation 4, we obtain twice as many estimates than if we would multiply only by L.

The coefficient $\lambda(K)$ is used as a smoothing device of the spectral estimates and is described as a lag window. This is used in order to reduce the variance of the sample spec-

Table 1: Spectral Analysis of Homicide Rates, United States, 1963-1974 (Monthly Data)

PERIOD P (MTHS)	FREQUENCY Wj	SPECTRAL DENSITY f(Wi)
∞	0.0069	0.0740
144.0	0.0069	0.0794
72.0	0.0139	0.0951
48.0	0.0208	0.1181
36.0	0.0278	0.1438
28.8	0.0347	0.1705
24.0	0.0417	0.2122
20.5	0.0486	0.3058
18.0	0.0556	0.4962
16.0	0.0625	0.7923
14.4	0.0694	1.1299
13.0	0.0764	1.3861
12.0	0.0833	1.4539
11.0	0.0903	1.3224
10.2	0.0972	1.0867
9.6	0.1042	0.8781
9.0	0.1111	0.7738
8.4	0.1181	0.7682
8.0	0.1250	0.8192
7.5	0.1319	0.9126
7.2	0.1389	1.0735
6.8	0.1458	1.3183
6.5	0.1528	1.6011
6.2	0.1597	1.8156
6.0	0.1667	1.8574
5.7	0.1736	1.6958
5.5	0.1806	1.3965
5.3	0.1875	1.0820
5.1	0.1944	0.8620
4.9	0.2014	0.7875
4.8	0.2083	0.8531
4.6	0.2153	1.0416
4.5	0.2222	1.3655
4.3	0.2292	1.8615
4.2	0.2361	2.5282
4.1	0.2431	3.2548
4.0	0.2500	3.8200
3.8	0.2569	3.9937
3.7	0.2639	3.6784
3.6	0.2708	2.9806
3.6	0.2778	2.1538
3.5	0.2847	1.4677
3.4	0.2917	1.1080
3.3	0.2986	1.1550
3.2	0.3056	1.6044
3.2	0.3125	2.3729
3.1	0.3194	2.8869
3.0	0.3264	4.1029
3.0	0.3333	4.5845
2.9	0.3403	4.6054
2.8	0.3472	4.2080
2.8	0.3542	3.5737
2.7	0.3611	2.9243
2.7	0.3681	2.4189
2.6	0.3750	2.1207
2.6	0.3819	2.0493
2.5	0.3889	2.2556
2.5	0.3958	2.8214
2.4	0.4028	3.7551
2.4	0.4097	4.8710
2.4	0.4167	5.7913
2.3	0.4236	6.1197
2.3	0.4306	5.6745
2.2	0.4375	4.6034
2.2	0.4444	3.2917
2.2	0.4514	2.1403
2.1	0.4583	1.3786
2.1	0.4653	1.0194
2.1	0.4722	0.9388
2.0	0.4792	0.9893
2.0	0.4861	1.0677
2.0	0.4931	1.1249
2.0	0.5000	1.1449

tral density function. In this chapter the Parazan window was used. The formula for λ(K) is presented as follows:

$$
\lambda(K) = \begin{cases} 1 - \dfrac{6K^2}{L^2}\left(1 - \dfrac{K}{L}\right), & 0 \leqslant K \leqslant \dfrac{L}{2} \\[2ex] 2\left(1 - \dfrac{K}{L}\right)^3 & \dfrac{L}{2} \leqslant K \leqslant L \end{cases} \qquad [5]
$$

The lag values K vary between 0 and L where L is the truncation point for calculating the A.C.F. values. A detailed discussion on lag windows in spectral analysis can be found in Jenkins and Watts (1968).

Table 1 represents the estimated values of the spectral density function of homicide rates for the time period January 1963 to December 1974 for the United States. The graphical presentation of the spectral density estimates will assist in identifying the various peaks of the spectral density function. Generally, substantial peaks in the spectrum for a given frequency is indicative of the substantial contribution to the variance explained by the statistical model. Similarly, if there are no substantial cyclical components, the spectrum is flat, meaning that no particular cycle contributes significantly to explaining the variance. The highest peak was observed for the frequency of 0.4236 which is equivalent to 2.36 months. However, if we consider the seasonal variation as composed of 6 components (using months as the time unit), the following frequencies should be considered 1/12, 1/6, 1/4, 1/3, 5/12 (see Granger and Hatanaka, 1964: 215). These frequencies correspond to the period of 12, 6, 4, 3, 2.4, and 2 months. Examination of Table 1 will reveal that the peaks of the spectral density function occurred at these particular frequencies or at their immediate neighborhood. Hence, the first conclusion is that homicide rates, when examined on a time series basis, reflect strong seasonal variations. The second conclusion is that at 95% confidence levels, peaks occurred in the spectral density function that at short time periods—e.g., 2.4 and 3 months—were statistically significant.[2] This conclusion was also reported by McPheters and Stronge (1974). They interpreted the short cycles of the crime of assault in the following way: "A singly violent crime may touch off a series of imitations which rise to a peak in frequency of occurrence and then taper off until another violent crime receives major publicity" (McPheters and Stronge, 1974: 337). Furthermore, they suggest that short period cycles of crimes are dominated by short-run considerations such as weather conditions, time of year, and the like.

The empirical findings that homicide is affected by short-run considerations weaken the possibility of identifying a causal nexus between monthly economic changes and homicide rates. Numerous economic researches utilizing spectral analysis reported that economic time series are characterized by "long swing" considerations (see Granger and Hatanaka, 1964). Jonish and Worthley (1973) studied the cyclical behavior of unemployment and help-wanted index. This study reported that the highest peaks of the spectral density values were observed for the frequencies 0, 1/12, and 1/6, which suggests "long swing" cycles. Cross-spectral analysis between unemployment and help-wanted index revealed high coherency values for the two series at the same frequencies.

An important methodological consideration in conducting spectral analysis is the length of the time series. Short time series could lead to an incomplete and distorted picture of the derived spectral estimates.[3] In order to validate our findings for the time series 1963-1974, the homicide rate series were extended to cover the period 1940-1974 (monthly data). Spectral analysis of this time series reconfirmed the previous findings with the following exceptions: (1) a significant peak was observed at the frequency 0.35 which is equivalent to 2.85 months; (2) low frequencies such as 1/12 and 1/6 revealed no significant peaks.[4] These findings support the general conclusions that homicide rates are characterized by short-term cycles.

In the second stage of this study, an attempt was made to identify the annual cycles of homicide rates. For this

Table 2: Spectral Analysis of Homicide Rates, United States, 1900-1974 (Yearly Data)

PERIOD P (YRS)	FREQUENCY Wj	SPECTRAL DENSITY	
∞	0.	5.2977	
72.0	0.0139	5.0887	
36.0	0.0278	4.5350	
24.0	0.0417	3.8108	
18.0	0.0556	3.0949	
14.4	0.0694	2.5044	
12.0	0.0833	2.0915	
10.2	0.0972	1.8741	
9.0	0.1111	1.8470	
8.0	0.1250	1.9697	
7.2	0.1389	2.1613	
6.5	0.1528	2.3278	
6.0	0.1667	2.4026	
5.5	0.1806	2.3677	
5.1	0.1944	2.2462	
4.8	0.2083	2.0802	
4.5	0.2222	1.9108	
4.2	0.2361	1.7628	
4.0	0.2500	1.6390	
3.7	0.2639	1.5308	
3.6	0.2778	1.4399	
3.4	0.2917	1.3897	
3.2	0.3056	1.4048	
3.1	0.3194	1.4774	
3.0	0.3333	1.5578	
2.8	0.3472	1.5851	
2.7	0.3611	1.5299	
2.6	0.3750	1.4088	
2.5	0.3889	1.2644	
2.4	0.4028	1.1374	
2.4	0.4167	1.0568	
2.3	0.4306	1.0410	
2.2	0.4444	1.0959	
2.1	0.4583	1.2065	
2.1	0.4722	1.3355	
2.0	0.4861	1.4372	
2.0	0.5000	1.4756	

analysis, data were available only since 1900. Hence, since we have only 74 observations, the interpretation of this series is only tentative. The A.C.F. and spectral analysis based on annual data are presented in Table 2.

From Figure 2 and Table 2, we can observe that the A.C.F. and the spectrum are relatively flat. The only small peak observed was for frequency 0.1667 which corresponds to a 6-year cycle. This coefficient was only marginally significant at the 95% confidence level. The high spectral density of frequency 0 might suggest that the series is not stationary, however, the examination of the A.C.F. of this series revealed that the autocorrelation damped out by N/4, which suggests a stationary series when the transformation of first differences $\Delta Z_t = Z_t - Z_{t-1}$ took place. The lack of significant peaks at the annual level is consistent with the general interpretation that no "long swing" cycles are observed for homicide rates. Nevertheless, the interpretation should be handled cautiously because of the short nature of the time series under investigation.

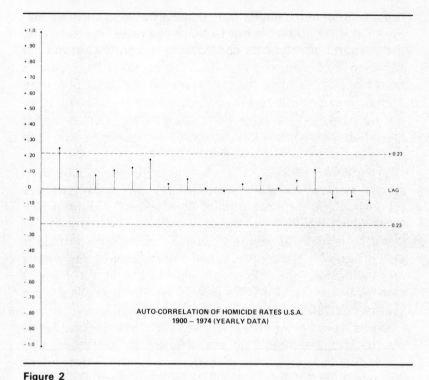

AUTO-CORRELATION OF HOMICIDE RATES U.S.A.
1900 – 1974 (YEARLY DATA)

Figure 2

Homicide and Leading Economic Indicators

In a previous section of this chapter it was shown that homicide rates manifest "short swings" or "short runs" which mean that the highest contribution of the spectrum power occurs in high frequencies, e.g., 0.4236, 0.3403 and so on. On the other hand, economic series are characterized by "long swing" cycles. Hamermesh (1969) provides ample evidence of the nature of economic time series. By analyzing 112 economic series (layoffs, new hires, quits, and output change), based on 28 different industries, it was shown that with the exception of output change all the other economic indicators were characterized by a concentration of the spectrum power in the lower frequencies (see also Klotz and Neal, 1973).

Given this evidence, a research effort to identify economic leading indicators that could "explain" the cyclical variation of homicide rates does not seem to be promising. However, the evidence from past economic research does not automatically imply that economic time cannot "explain" the cyclical behavior of homicide rates. For example, the researcher might be considering a significant time lag between economic changes and the occurrence of violent behavior. Furthermore, most past analyses of economic time series were performed on aggregate indicators which does not rule out the possibility that "short swing" cycles can be identified in economic time series broken down by age, race and sex, and the like.

In light of this view, a cross spectral analysis was conducted on the following variables: (1) unemployment rate for males 20-24—seasonally unadjusted,[5] (2) homicide rates—monthly data for the period 1963-1974. It was decided to select the unemployment rate for this particular age group (20-24) on the evidence provided by numerous criminological research which indicates that the highest rate of homicide offenders occurs in this age group (see Wolfgang, 1958: 65-78).

Cross spectral analysis attempts to find the statistical relationship between two stationary time series. In this study we consider unemployed rate as the independent variable X_t and homicide rate as the dependent variable Y_t. By conducting cross spectral analysis, the following could be achieved.

(1) The cyclical components of each series could be identified over a range of given frequencies or time periods.
(2) The degree of association between the cycles of the two time series could be established for a given range of frequencies.
(3) The lead lag relationship between the cycles of the two series could be established for a given range of frequencies.

The result of the cross spectral analysis is presented in Table 3. The table presents the coherency and phase shift for a given frequency or time period. The coherency can be interpreted as a squared correlation, r^2. This coefficient varies between 0 and 1.0. For example, if we conduct a cross spectral analysis of two identical time series, X_t and X_t, we will find that the coherency value is 1.0 for all fre-

Table 3: Cross Spectral Analysis of Unemployment Rates Males 20-24 and Homicide Rates, United States, 1963-1974 (Monthly Data)

LAG	FREQUENCY	TIME PERIOD (Months)	COHERENCE	TIME LAG Phase(Deg)	Months
1	0.01389	72.00000	0.26069	7.47	1.50
2	0.02778	36.00000	0.22757	3.77	0.38
3	0.04167	24.00000	0.23176	-16.32	-1.09
4	0.05556	18.00000	0.55965	-22.73	-1.13
5	0.06944	14.40000	0.74999	-18.38	-0.73
6	0.08333	12.00000	0.76564	-16.06	-0.53
7	0.09722	10.28571	0.60098	-15.04	-0.42
8	0.11111	9.00000	0.23468	-12.23	-0.30
9	0.12500	8.00000	0.03697	-1.10	-0.02
10	0.13889	7.20000	0.05919	19.57	0.40
11	0.15278	6.54545	0.31588	15.02	0.28
12	0.16667	6.00000	0.60015	12.73	0.21
13	0.18056	5.53846	0.71565	14.67	0.22
14	0.19444	5.14286	0.60882	25.29	0.37
15	0.20833	4.80000	0.29338	37.51	0.50
16	0.22222	4.50000	0.13916	22.61	0.29
17	0.23611	4.23529	0.28626	13.36	0.16
18	0.25000	4.00000	0.32856	9.98	0.11
19	0.26389	3.78947	0.19906	5.01	0.06
20	0.27778	3.60000	0.02433	-10.40	-0.10
21	0.29167	3.42857	0.05970	3.80	0.03
22	0.30556	3.27273	0.08575	-38.69	-0.36
23	0.31944	3.13043	0.04638	-81.07	-0.70
24	0.33333	3.00000	0.01103	19.16	0.16
25	0.34722	2.88000	0.05309	-51.89	-0.41
26	0.36111	2.76923	0.06696	-72.27	-0.56
27	0.37500	2.66667	0.00700	79.27	0.59
28	0.38889	2.57143	0.08629	-35.21	-0.26
29	0.40278	2.48276	0.34292	-23.24	-0.17
30	0.41667	2.40000	0.36518	-16.99	-0.11
31	0.43056	2.32258	0.23996	-15.12	-0.10
32	0.44444	2.25000	0.06869	-25.64	-0.17
33	0.45833	2.18182	0.00990	47.77	0.29
34	0.47222	2.11765	0.01466	-88.54	-0.52
35	0.48611	2.05714	0.04002	47.10	0.27
36	0.50000	2.00000	0.02495	0.00	0.00

quencies. The phase shift identifies the lead lag relationship between the cycles of unemployment and homicide rates.[6] From Table 3 it is evident that the high coherency (correlation) between unemployment rate for males 20-24 and homicide rates occurred only at tne low frequencies or where the two series manifested long cycles,[7] in particular, at the 12 and 6 month cycles. However, for high frequencies especially at the range where homicide rates indicated significant peaks of the spectral density function, the two series were found to be weakly correlated. The highest spectral density value of unemployment rate occurred at the frequency of 0.25 which is equivalent to a cycle of 4 months. However, at this particular point the spectral density value for homicide rates reached only a moderate value (see Table 1). It should also be noted that the point where two series were highly correlated (coherency of 0.77 for k = 6 or a 12-month cycle), homicide rates were leading unemployment rates by 0.7 month which suggest almost an instantaneous relationship between the two series at that particular frequency.[8]

Forecasting Model for Homicide Rates

In a previous section of this chapter the behavior of the time series of homicide rates was studied in the frequency domain. Generally, if we are interested in constructing a forecasting model, we have to work in the time domain. Hence, essentially we study the series as a sequence of observations in time. The frequency and time domain analysis can be considered as two complementary approaches in time series analyses.

Recent developments in building forecasting models is attributed to the work of Box and Jenkins (1968, 1970). In this section we will concentrate only on univariate forecasting models since no significant leading indicator was identified to assist us in optimizing the forecasting model. The univariate forecasting approach is based on the contention that by close examination of the history of the time series we could build a model which closely describes the behavior of the time series. It is beyond the scope of this chapter to discuss the technique in detail. (The interested reader should refer to Box and Jenkins, 1968, 1970.) The application of this technique in sociological research can be found in Vigderhous (1977).

The general class of forecasting model is identified as the ARMA model which is an abbreviation for Auto-Regressive Moving Average models. This model of the order (p,q) is

$$Z_t = \phi_1 Z_{t-1} + \phi_2 Z_{t-2} \ldots + \phi_p Z_{t-p} + a_t \tag{6}$$

$$- \theta_1 a_{t-1} - \theta_2 a_{t-2} \ldots - \theta_q a_{t-q}$$

where

$Z_t = Y_t - \mu$

a_t = random shocks "white noise" observed at time t

ϕ_i = weights applied to past data in the autoregressive model

θ_i = weights applied to previous shocks (forecast errors) in the moving average model.

The Autoregressive component of order p AR(P) of the forecasting model suggests an observed value at time t can be represented as a linear combination of its past values. This can be presented by the following equation:

$$Z_t = \phi_1 Z_{t-1} + \phi_2 Z_{t-2} + \ldots + \phi_p Z_{t-p} + a_t. \tag{7}$$

The value a_t is the unexplained portion of the model forecasting error or random shock. The Moving Average Component of the model or order q MA(q) suggests that a given observation at time t can be expressed in terms of linear combinations of present and past random shocks or forecasting errors. This component or the model can be described as follows:

$$Z_t = a_t - \theta_1 a_{t-1} - \theta_2 a_{t-2} \ldots - \theta_q a_{t-q}. \tag{8}$$

In building a forecasting model the A.C.F. should be examined, whereby significant spikes of the A.C.F. should be identified for constructing the model. For example, large spikes at time lags 1 and 2 suggest a moving average model of order 2 MA(2).

$$Z_t = a_t - \theta_1 a_{t-1} - \theta_2 a_{t-2}. \qquad [9]$$

This model suggests that the level of homicide at time t can be determined from the forecasting errors or random shocks at time t–1 and t–2 by using the appropriate weights θ_1 and θ_2 which have to be estimated. A significant advantage in using the Box-Jenkins technique is that forecasting errors are taken into consideration in order to optimize the forecast. Building a forecasting model is an iterative procedure where four basic steps are required: (1) Model Identification from the A.C.F., (2) Model Estimation, (3) Diagnostic Checking, and (4) Forecasting. The procedure requires testing of several plausible models and the final choice will depend on various statistical criteria. The most important one is that the time series will be stationary and that the residuals or forecasting errors will constitute a random process. Generally, a model which will minimize the forecasting errors will be selected given that it will meet other statistical criteria. (For details on diagnostic checking see Box and Jenkins, 1970.)

The final model of forecasting homicide rates takes the following form:

$$(1-\phi_{12}B^{12})(1-B)Z_t = (1-\theta_1 B)a_t \qquad [10]$$

where B is the backshift operator and ∇ is the first differencing of Z_t

$$B^m Z_t = Z_{t-m} \qquad \text{e.g.} \begin{cases} B^2 a_t = a_{t-2} \\ B^{12} a_t = a_{t-12} \\ \nabla Z_t = Z_t - Z_{t-1}. \end{cases}$$

Table 4: Parameter Estimation for Homicide Rate Monthly Data, 1963-1974

N = 144

PARAMETER NUMBER	PARAMETER TYPE	PARAMETER ORDER	ESTIMATED VALUE	95 PERCENT CONFIDENCE LEVEL	
				Lower Limit	Upper Limit
1	Seasonal Autoregressive	12	0.5632	0.4221	0.7043
2	Regular Autoregressive	1	0.7195	0.5927	0.8464

```
Residuals Mean Square    = 6.02539
Degrees of Freedom       = 129
Number of Residuals      = 131
Residual Standard Error  = 0.05039
```

Test White Noise X^2 = 24.83 p>.05 (Residuals can be considered as a random process)

NOTE: First differencing log values.

The forecasting model when simplified can be written as follows:

$$Z_t = Z_{t-1} + \phi_{12} Z_{t-12} - \phi_{12} Z_{t-13} + a_t - \theta_1 a_{t-1}. \qquad [11]$$

The estimates of this model are presented in Table 4. All the estimates presented in the table were found to be statistically significant at the 95% confidence level. For forecasting purposes, given the estimates, we can write the final model as follows:

$$Z_t = Z_{t-1} + 0.5632 Z_{t-12} - 0.5632 Z_{t-13} + a_t - 0.7195 a_{t-1}. \qquad [12]$$

The actual forecasted values of homicide rates are presented in Table 5. This table provides backward and forward forecasting. Hence, after the forecasting model was established it was tested by forecasting backward to the last 12 months of 1974 and 12 months ahead for 1975. The model should not be evaluated only in terms of its percent deviation from the actual but also in terms of the width of the confidence limits. For example, it is suggested that for January 1974, the actual value will be at the 95% confidence limit between 8.94 and 10.44. If forecasting is desired, then one should establish his forecast from the

Table 5: Forecasting Monthly Homicide Rates for the United States for the Period January 1974-December 1975

YEAR	MONTH	CONFIDENCE LIMITS 95%		ACTUAL	FORECAST	% ERROR FROM Actual
		Lower	Upper			
1974	January	8.68	10.79	9.90	9.68	- 1.36
"	February	8.69	10.90	9.30	9.74	- 4.73
"	March	8.92	11.27	10.0	10.03	- 3.00
"	April	8.68	11.05	9.20	9.80	- 6.12
"	May	8.49	10.90	8.30	9.62	-15.90
"	June	8.76	11.33	10.00	9.97	0.3
"	July	9.03	11.75	10.30	10.31	- .097
"	August	8.70	11.41	10.90	9.97	8.53
"	September	8.77	11.58	10.60	10.09	4.81
"	October	8.49	11.29	10.60	9.80	7.54
"	November	8.66	11.59	11.40	10.03	12.01
"	December	8.88	11.94	11.30	10.31	8.76
1975*	January	8.31	11.78	10.5	9.90	5.71
"	February	8.28	11.89	10.4	9.94	4.42
"	March	8.37	12.16	10.3	10.10	1.94
"	April	8.21	12.07	9.7	9.97	- 2.78
"	May	8.07	12.02	9.7	9.87	- 1.75
"	June	8.19	12.33	10.1	10.07	0.297
"	July	8.31	12.63	10.0	10.26	- 2.6
"	August	8.10	12.46	10.2	10.07	1.27
"	September	8.11	12.60	10.3	10.13	1.65
"	October	7.94	12.47	9.6	9.97	- 3.85
"	November	8.00	12.69	9.6	10.10	- 5.20
"	December	8.09	12.95	9.5	10.26	- 8.00

*The data for 1975 were received upon personal communication with U.S. Department of Health, Education and Welfare. All other statistics are based on official published homicide rates.

last data point available (e.g., December 1974 should be used as the starting point for forecast). The Box-Jenkins technique cannot forecast the turning point or a sudden change. It is evident that from August 1974 to December 1974 the percent error from the actual values is substantial. These values were deviating significantly from the general seasonal trend. It is therefore interesting to identify various factors which cause a sudden increase in homicide rates.

CONCLUSIONS

This chapter provided a systematic time series analysis of homicide rates in the time and frequency domain. The major purpose of the frequency domain analysis (spectral and cross spectral analysis) was to identify the cyclical variations of homicide rates and their relationship to cyclical variations of unemployment rates. It was demonstrated that homicide rates are characterized by significant seasonal movements. However, such movements are significantly associated with seasonal cyclical variations of unemployment rates for only "long swing" cycles (e.g., 12 and 6 months cycles). The findings generally support previous cross sectional and cross cultural research which were found to be weak or nonsignificant associations between economic changes and serious crimes (see Thomas, 1925; Ogburn, 1923, Phelps, 1929; Sutherland, 1974; Krohn, 1976). The analysis of homicide rates in the time domain aimed to demonstrate that the empirical knowledge of the behavior of time series could be utilized in constructing a forecasting model.

The systematic analysis of time series of crime rates could reveal interesting results which could direct future research in identifying the socioeconomic and demographic correlates of crime rates. The knowlege of the cyclical variations of homicide rates could direct the search in identifying various determinants of crime rates. The analysis presented in this chapter suggests that economic time series could not be considered as significant determinants of variations in homicide rates. However, cross spectral analysis could be more meaningful if data were available on unemployment broken down by age and race. The conclusions presented here should be considered as tentative and should be examined in future research.

Time series analysis of crime rates is an interesting and promising area in criminological research. There is much more to learn about variations of serious crimes beyond the obvious such as identification of a general trend or percent increase in such crimes over time.

NOTES

1. Further information on these studies and others can be found in Curtis (1974: 183-221).

2. A test of significance was conducted to determine whether the identified peaks in the spectral density functions or spectrum are statistically significant (see also Jenkins and Watts, 1968: 255). In other words, we have to determine whether the series is different from a random series or statistically different from a "white noise" process. The confidence interval of the estimated spectrum is determined as follows:

$$\log \hat{f}(w_i) + \log \frac{V}{\chi_v\left(1 - \frac{\alpha}{2}\right)} \;,\; \log \hat{f}(w_i) + \log \frac{V}{\chi_v(\alpha/2)}$$

where V is the respective degrees of freedom which is computed for the Parazan window as follows: $V = (3.71)(N/V)$ χ_v^2 = the theoretical chi-square value for the respective degrees of freedom V and α is the confidence level.

3. Klotz and Neal (1973) suggested that a large number of observations are required in order to identify low frequencies to be statistically significant. They suggested a lower bound of 75 observations in practice.

4. Different choice of the lag number L which varied between 15%-25% of the observation did not alter the major findings reported in Table 1.

5. The data for seasonally unadjusted unemployment rates for males 20-24 were obtained by personal communications with the U.S. Department of Labor, Labor Statistics. These data are not published in official reports and were extracted from Current Population Survey.

6. Analysis of lead lag relationship intends to identify in this case whether unemployment precedes homicide or visa versa. From a theoretical point of view, it is expected that changes in unemployment rates will produce changes in homicide rates given a certain time lag between the two variables. However, this procedure does not establish a causal relationship since both cycles could be affected by a third cycle.

7. The cross-correlation function was used to align the series. Jenkins and Watts (1968) have shown that the estimates of the coherency and phase values may be biased if the time series are not aligned. In this study the highest cross-correlation between unemployment and homicide rates occurred at K = 6 where $r_{xy} = 0.38$. Hence, the series was aligned such that the peak in the cross-correlation function the aligned series occurred at K = 0.

8. The lead lag relationships generally have to be interpreted cautiously (see Hause, 1971). Particularly, such interpretations will depend on the condition that the high coherency values between the two series are observed.

REFERENCES

BOX, G.E.P. and G. M. JENKINS (1970) Time Series Analysis: Forecasting and Control. San Francisco: Holden Day.

———— (1968) "Some recent advances in forecasting and control, part I." Applied Statistics 17: 91-109.

CHAN, H. and J. HAYYA (1976) "Spectral analysis in business forecasting." Decision Sciences 7: 137-151.

CURTIS, L. A. (1974) Criminal Violence: National Patterns and Behavior. Toronto: Lexington Books.

ELWIN, V. (1943) Maria Murder and Suicide. London: Oxford Univ. Press.

FARLEY, J. U. and M. J. HINICH (1969) "Marketing applications of spectral analysis." Proceedings Fall Conference, American Marketing Association.

FISHMAN, G. S. (1969) Spectral Methods in Econometrics. Cambridge: Harvard Univ. Press.

GRANGER, C. W. and M. HATANAKA (1964) Spectral and Analysis of Economic Time Series. Princeton: Princeton Univ. Press.

HAMERMESH, D. S. (1969) "Spectral analysis of the relation between gross employment changes and output changes 1958-1966." Rev. of Economics and Statistics 51: 62-69.

HAUSE, J. (1971) "Spectral analysis and the detection of lend-lag relations." Amer. Economic Rev. 61: 213-217.

JENKINS, G. M. and D. G. WATTS (1968) Spectral Analysis and Its Applications. San Francisco: Holden Day.

JONISH, J. E. and R. G. WORTHLEY (1973) "Cyclical behavior of unemployment and help wanted index: a cross spectral analysis." Decision Sciences 4: 350-363.

KLOTZ, B. A. and L. NEAL (1973) "Spectral and cross spectral analysis of the long-swing hypothesis." Rev. of Economics and Statistics 55: 291-298.

KROHN, M. D. (1976) "Inequality unemployment and crime: a cross-national analysis." Soc. Q. 17: 303-313.

MacKAY, D. B. (1973) "A spectral analysis of the frequency of supermarket visits." J. of Marketing Research 10: 84-90.

McPHETERS, L. R. and W. B. STRONGE (1974) "Spectral analysis of reported crime data." J. of Criminal Justice 2: 329-344.

MAYER, T. F. and W. R. ARNEY (1974) "Spectral analysis and the study of social change," pp. 309-355 in H. L. Costner (ed.) Sociological Methodology 1973-1974. San Francisco: Jossey-Bass.

OGBURN, W. F. (1923) "Business fluctuations as social forces." Social Forces 1: 73-78.

PHELPS, H. A. (1929) "Cycles of Crime." J. of Criminal Law and Criminology 20: 107-112.

SUTHERLAND, G. D. (1974) Principles of Criminology. Philadelphia: Lippincott.

TARDIFF, G. (1966) "La criminalité de violence." Master's thesis, University of Montreal. (unpublished)

THOMAS, D. S. (1925) Social Aspects of Business Cycle: 143-144. London: Routledge & Kegan Paul.

VIGDERHOUS, G. (1977) "Forecasting sociological phenomena: implications of Box-Jenkins Methodology to suicide rates," in K. F. Schuessler (ed.) Sociological Methodology 1978. San Francisco: Jossey-Bass.

WOLFGANG, M. E. (1958) Patterns in Criminal Homicide. Philadelphia: Univ. of Pennsylvania Press.

7

Lyle W. Shannon
*Iowa Urban Community
Research Center*

A LONGITUDINAL STUDY OF DELINQUENCY AND CRIME

This report is a brief overview of a longitudinal study of the relationship of juvenile delinquency to adult crime in Racine, Wisconsin.

To obtain the police contact data to which we shall refer, two cohorts were selected from the files of the Racine Unified School District, one of 1,352 persons born in 1942 and the other of 2,099 persons born in 1949, and followed through the files of the Juvenile Bureau and Records Division of the Racine Police Department. The second data set consists of responses to questions asked in lengthy interviews during the summer of 1976 with 333 persons from the 1942 cohort and 556 from the 1949 cohort. We shall, however, make only brief reference to the latter in this chapter.

Married names located in the Records Section of the Racine Health Department provided a basis for following females throughout their careers. Each person's length of residence in Racine (the period of time he/she was

AUTHOR'S NOTE: Prepared under Grant Numbers 76JN-99-0008 and 76JN-99-1005 from the National Institute for Juvenile Justice and Delinquency Prevention, Law Enforcement Assistance Administration, U.S. Department of Justice. Funds were also provided by the Max C. Fleischmann Foundation. Points of view or opinions in this document are those of the author and do not necessarily represent the official position or policies of the U.S. Department of Justice or the Max C. Fleischmann Foundation.

at risk in the community) was determined insofar as possible through reference to City Directories and telephone directories and was continued by telephone contact with family and friends during the interviewing phase for anyone whose presence had not already been established. Persons with continuous residence are those missing no more than three years between the age of 6 and June 1, 1974, the cut-off date for data collection. Depending on the type of analysis involved we have utilized either entire cohorts or only those persons with continuous residence.[1]

The police contact data include I.D., age, and residence of alleged offender, type of complainant, place of contact, type of contact, seriousness of contact, police disposition, and a variety of other pertinent pieces of data about the composition of the group if it was a group offense, and so on.

As in similar studies, a small number of persons was responsible for a disproportionately large number of all police contacts in both cohorts. Of those from the 1942 cohort with continuous residence in Racine, 5.0% were responsible for 41.4% of the contacts and 7.3% for 50.6% of the contacts. Concentration was slightly greater in the 1949 cohort, where 5.1% were responsible for 44.5% of the contacts and 7.0% for 51.6%.

THE SPATIAL DISTRIBUTION
OF PERSONS WITH CONTACTS

Where one lives while growing up may be considered a factor in determining whether or not one will have contacts with the police at that and later stages in life. The 26 residential subareas (shown on Map 1) may be reduced to five Natural Areas. They are shown in computer contoured form on Map 2.

Maps 3 and 4, showing the average number of contacts generated by the members of each cohort from age 6 to June 1974, according to their most frequent area of residence during the ages 6 through 17, are presented in order to assist in visualizing the relationship of residential areas, as indicators of socioeconomic status areas, to

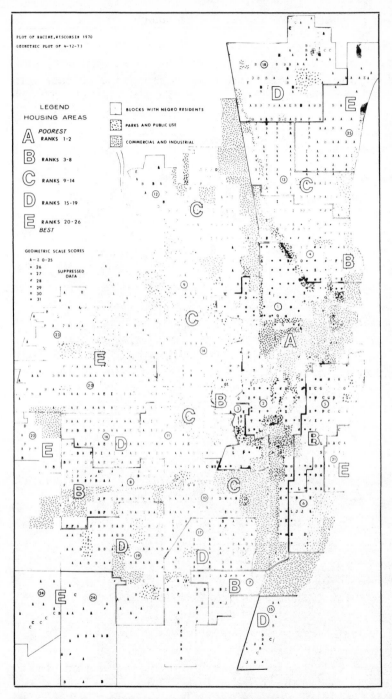

MAP 1: NATURAL AREAS OF RACINE (Based on 1970 Census of Housing Data)

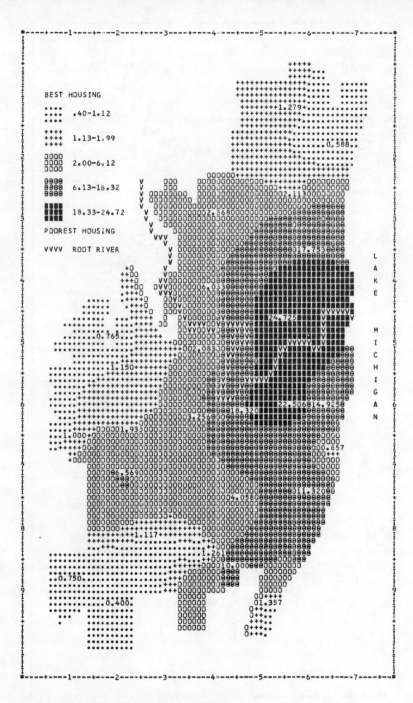

MAP 2: NATURAL AREAS OF RACINE (Based on 1970 Census of Housing Data Average Geometric Scores of 26 Areas)

the areas in which careers in delinquency and crime develop as measured by police contacts. The shape of each
contoured area is based on the average rate of each of the
26 subareas at their central points on the assumption
that rates are not the same throughout each natural area
but gradually change toward the rates of adjacent natural
areas. Thus, through computer construction of isopleths
utilizing centroids, we are able to better communicate
a picture of residential areas and the distribution of average
police contact rates. Differences in the pattern of total
contact rates are evident between the 1942 and 1949
cohorts.

If we assume that some of the classic sociological explanations of delinquency and crime have merit, i.e., that
delinquency and crime are generated at lower rates in
areas least favorable to crime, then the proportions of
each race/ethnic group with police contacts should be
similar to each other in each natural area. If these proportions are the same or very similar it becomes difficult to
give credence to the oversimplified race/ethnic explanations which, although interred many years ago, linger
and are still given considerable weight by a sociologically
unsophisticated segment of the population. If these proportions are not similar, the problem still remains of how
to account for race/ethnic variation in juvenile delinquency
and crime.

For those males who resided in the innner city (Area
A) most of the time during the ages 6 through 17, a higher
proportion of blacks in the 1942 cohort had police contacts
than did whites at every age period (see Table 1). There
were too few Chicanos and blacks who grew up outside
Area A for comparision with whites in these areas. However, considering the facts that such a large proportion of
the cohort (basically a white cohort) was located outside
the inner city, that 84% of the white males had police
contacts at one time or another, and that over three-fourths
of the Anglos from the highest socioeconomic status area
had at least one police contact, it cannot be said that delinquency and crime in the cohort were either a black problem
or only a problem of those who resided in the inner city.

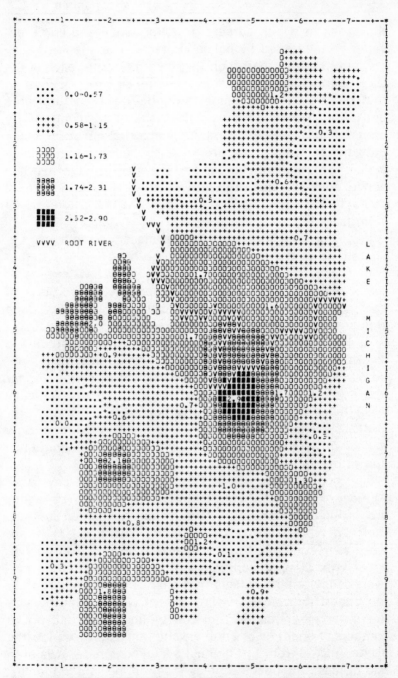

MAP 3: AVERAGE NUMBER OF POLICE CONTACTS PER PERSON IN 1942 BIRTH COHORT AGE 6-31 (BY AREA OF RESIDENCE AGE 6-17) NATURAL AREAS CONTOURED

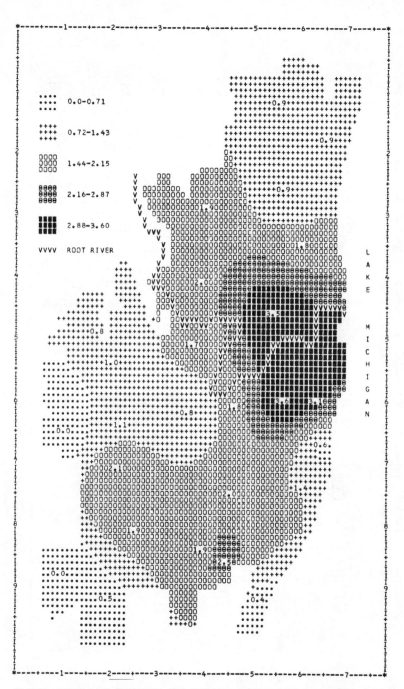

MAP 4: AVERAGE NUMBER OF POLICE CONTACTS PER PERSON IN 1949 BIRTH COHORT AGE 6-25 (BY AREA OF RESIDENCE AGE 6-17) NATURAL AREAS CONTOURED

Table 1: Percent with Police Contacts Among Cohort Members with Continuous Racine Residence by Race/Ethnicity and Natural Area of Juvenile Residence

Natural Areas, Lower (Inner-City) to Higher Quality Housing*

	A			B			C	D	E	Combinations** A,B,C,D,E			Total		
	A	MA	N	A	MA	N	A	A	A	A	MA	N	A	MA	N
[1949 cohort, Males]															
Contacts 6-17	62	0	69	64	0	0	64	49	48	45	0	100	56	0	75
Contacts 18-20	45	50	85	55	0	0	47	45	55	54	0	100	44	33	87
Contacts 21+	73	100	92	67	100	0	76	67	65	67	0	100	70	100	93
Contacts Ever	81	100	100	84	100	0	89	90	78	77	0	100	84	100	100
N	57	2	15	81	1	0	78	49	23	70	0	2	338	3	15
[1949 cohort, Females]															
Contacts 6-17	20	0	0	15	0	50	15	25	27	20	0	0	19	0	25
Contacts 18-20	20	0	0	15	33	100	11	15	9	11	0	0	14	0	50
Contacts 21+	50	0	100	25	67	100	29	36	36	29	0	100	31	20	100
Contacts Ever	50	0	100	45	67	100	45	52	55	44	0	100	48	40	100
N	39	1	1	55	3	2	56	51	22	66	1	1	267	5	4
[1942 cohort, Males]															
Contacts 6-17	64	88	87	65	80	33	70	60	84	48	100	100	64	87	83
Contacts 18-20	65	65	81	49	80	33	51	46	33	49	100	50	48	73	76
Contacts 21+	61	75	84	55	80	33	50	49	29	46	100	50	48	80	79
Contacts Ever	88	100	97	82	100	33	85	78	74	77	100	100	81	100	93
N	59	8	57	150	5	3	145	139	77	107	2	2	677	15	42
[1942 cohort, Females]															
Contacts 6-17	36	33	61	22	33	45	53	24	24	18	0	50	27	33	56
Contacts 18-20	53	67	50	28	33	29	21	23	28	22	0	25	25	44	44
Contacts 21+	17	33	54	24	33	29	19	22	22	21	0	25	22	33	46
Contacts Ever	56	100	75	52	67	57	54	49	45	48	0	50	53	78	69
N	36	3	28	93	6	7	129	109	58	83	0	4	488	9	39

*Columns for minority groups have been eliminated when there were 4 or fewer persons in the natural area.

**Outside Racine and not ascertained included.

While disproportionate numbers of black males who resided in the inner city during the ages 6 through 17 in
the 1949 cohort, and less consistently Chicanos, had
police contacts at each stage in their careers and at all
stages combined, minority groups again made up only
a small proportion of the cohort, and even in Area A where
they constituted over 40% of the cohort in 1949 they did
not have such a larger percentage of persons in their group
who had police contacts than did the whites that they could
be defined as constituting the problem in that area.

Put differently (see Table 2), the race/ethnic proportion
of those males from areas of high delinquency and crime
who have had police contacts at some stage in their careers
is roughly the same as the race/ethnic proportion of those
who grew up in the areas of high delinquency and crime.
Of the 1942 males who grew up in Natural Area A, 71.2%
were whites and 66.7% of those males who had contacts
were also whites. The Chicano males made up 3.8% of
those who grew up in Area A but 4.4% of the males from
the area who had contacts. Black males in the cohort who
grew up in Area A made up 25.0% of the total males in
the area and 28.9% of the males with contacts. When
we turn to the males in Natural Area B, C, D, and E we
find that most of those from the 1942 cohort residing
there were whites, as were most of those with contacts.

Of the 1949 males who grew up in Natural Area A,
56.7% were whites as were 54.2% of the males with con-
tacks. Black males in the 1949 cohort constituted 35.6%
of those who grew up in Area A and 37.5% of those with
contacts. Chicanos made up 7.7% of the cohort from this
area and 8.3% of those with contacts. Delinquency and
crime continued to be a white phenomenon outside the
inner city for the 1949 cohort.

When police contacts were divided into traffic versus
nontraffic categories, essentially the same pattern pre-
vailed except that the proportion of blacks was somewhat
greater than whites in the nontraffic category than in
the traffic category.

In order to obtain a score representing the seriousness
of delinquent and criminal careers for each person in each

Table 2: Race/Ethnicity of 1942 and 1949 Cohort Members with Continuous Residence in Racine and Their Police Contacts Within Natural Areas of Principal Juvenile Residence, by Percent

	Area A: Inner-City		Areas B,C,D,E		Combinations* A,B,C,D,E		Total	
	1942	1949	1942	1949	1942	1949	1942	1949
MALES:								
Total who could have had contacts 6-21+								
Anglo	71.2	56.7	99.6	97.3	97.2	96.4	94.9	91.5
Mexican-American	3.8	7.7	0.4	1.7	0.0	1.8	0.8	2.6
Negro	25.0	35.6	0.0	1.0	2.8	1.8	4.2	5.9
	100.0	100.0	100.0	100.0	100.0	100.0	99.9	100.0
N	52	104	232	525	72	111	356	740
Contacts Ever 6-21+								
Anglo	66.7	54.2	99.5	97.2	96.4	95.3	94.0	90.1
Mexican-American	4.4	8.3	0.5	2.1	0.0	2.3	1.0	3.1
Negro	28.9	37.5	0.0	0.7	3.6	2.3	5.0	6.8
	100.0	100.0	100.0	100.0	100.0	99.9	100.0	100.0
N	45	96	200	423	56	86	301	605

Table 2 (Continued)

FEMALES:

Total who could have had contacts 6-21+

Anglo	95.1	54.5	96.4	96.5	97.1	97.6	96.4	91.7
Mexican-American	2.4	4.5	1.8	1.7	1.5	0.0	1.8	1.8
Negro	2.4	40.9	1.8	1.7	1.5	2.4	1.8	6.5
	99.9	99.9	100.0	99.9	100.1	100.0	100.0	100.0
N	41	66	168	403	68	85	277	554

Contacts ever 6-21+

Anglo	95.8	46.5	94.9	95.6	96.7	95.2	95.5	88.3
Mexican-American	0.0	7.0	2.5	2.4	0.0	0.0	1.5	2.7
Negro	4.2	46.5	2.5	1.9	3.3	4.8	3.0	8.9
	100.0	100.0	99.9	99.9	100.0	100.0	100.0	99.9
N	24	43	79	206	30	42	153	291

*Includes outside Racine and not ascertained.

cohort the 25 types of or reasons for police contact were first divided into six categories with weights ranging from 6 to 1 (felony against the person, 6; felony against property, 5; major misdemeanor, 4; minor misdemeanor, 3; juvenile condition, 2; contact for suspicion, investigation, or information, 1).[2] The number of contacts in each category was then multiplied by the appropriate weight for that category for each person. While this may seem to be a more or less arbitrary procedure, it is consistent with police reporting and the files of the Records Division of the Racine Police Department as to whether or not a specific act that resulted in a police contact was considered to be a felony or a misdemeanor.

In addition to variation in contact rates and seriousness by areas, there is the problem of sheer numbers, i.e., where were the people socialized who had the most frequent contacts with the police for the most serious reasons? Where were the behaviors learned that seem to generate disproportionately high numbers of police contacts for the most serious types of offenses?

To obtain the data used for Maps 5 and 6 the average seriousness score of individual careers in each area was multiplied by the number of persons in the cohort who grew up in that area and thus produced what we have designated as a grand seriousness score for each of the 26 subareas. While the 1942 cohort and 1949 cohort do not produce identical patterns, their similarity is noticeable. Both reveal that although delinquency and crime are widely dispersed, the inner city and its interstitial areas generate disproportional amounts of serious delinquency and crime, both as a consequence of high density and more serious reasons for police contacts.

THE HYPOTHESIS OF INCREASING SERIOUSNESS

We noted earlier that a large proportion of the police contacts for delinquency and crime are generated by a relatively small proportion of the population, and there is some evidence that lengthy careers include more serious

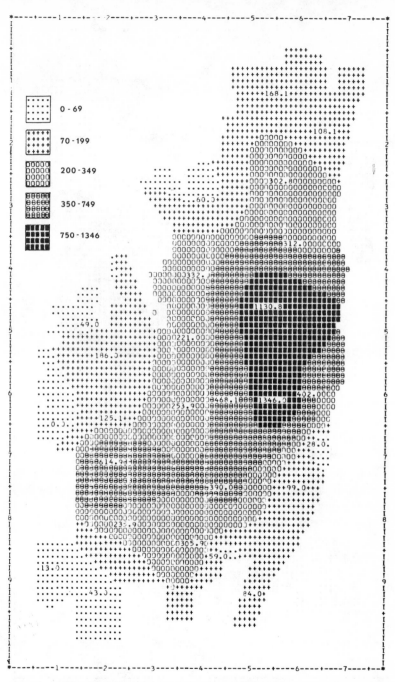

MAP 5: GRAND SERIOUSNESS SCORES OF POLICE CONTACTS FOR 1942 BIRTH COHORT AGE 6-31 (BY AREA OF RESIDENCE AGE 6-17)

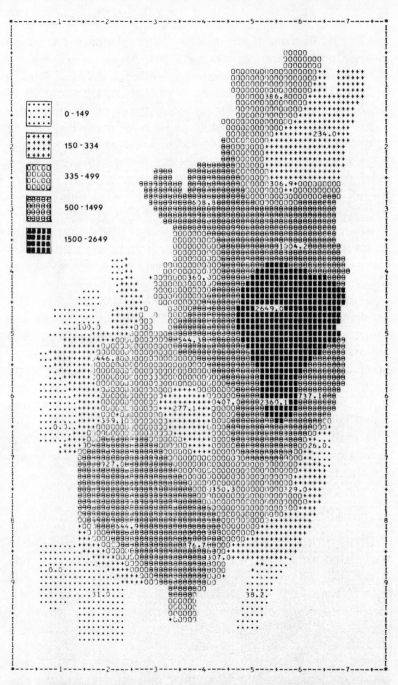

MAP 6: GRAND SERIOUSNESS SCORES OF POLICE CONTACTS FOR 1949 BIRTH COHORT AGE 6-25 (BY AREA OF RESIDENCE AGE 6-17)

kinds of offenses than do very short careers based on chance or sporadic contact with the police.

While a number of published case histories have served as a basis for the historical development of a model of delinquency as ever-increasing in seriousness over the years from its inception into adulthood, there have been few longitudinal studies with data adequate for a test of the model. The one test in which we have the most confidence, that conducted by Wolfgang et al. (1972), found little or no increase in severity of offenses from the first through the ninth offense.

When curves were drawn representing seriousness of contacts by contact order from the first to the Kth contact for each race/ethnic/sex group there was little evidence of progression for those with continuous residence in Racine. Since there was a certain amount of fluctuation in seriousness scores as contacts proceeded from the first to, say, the 96th contact for white males in the 1949 cohort, 5-contact moving averages were calculated for both cohorts. Even with the 5-contact moving average there was considerable fluctuation for black males but it would be risky to say that average seriousness scores have systematically increased for this group. The fact that traffic offenses increase with age at contact in each cohort and other offenses decline accounts to some extent for the flatness of the curve, however.

DIFFERENTIAL PATTERNS OF REFERRAL

Once the police contact an individual they must make a decision leading to disposition of the incident. They may decide to do nothing (release) or they may decide that formal disposition (of one sort or another) is required (referral). Referral rates are dependent upon the action of police and juvenile justice personnel whose attitudes and associated behavior may be influenced among other things by sensationalized events and expressed concerns of citizens' groups. At the point of referral, action may be intitiated which eventuates in highly disproportionate numbers of institutionalized minority group members and thus gives emphasis to race/ethnic explanations of delinquency and crime. Indeed, these data (as of June 1976, 32.8% of the population of juvenile institutions and 41.4% of the adult institutions of Wisconsin were nonwhite in a state that has less than 10% of its population nonwhite) suggest a racial explanation of delinquency and crime. To what extent is this explained by race/ethnicity and socioeconomic status and to what extent is it explained by police definitions of what should be done in response to the behavior that they encounter? May it be that the initial screening process, the decision to refer or not to refer, is the first step in a chain of events, each sending a few percent more of the minority groups or low socioeconomic status juveniles on to the next stage of the process?

The manner in which each police contact was disposed of at the time of contact or as a consequence of questioning in the Juvenile Bureau was coded according to the following categories: (1) contact, released; counselled, released; (2) referred to County Probation Department; (3) referred to County Welfare; (4) referred to State Department of Public Welfare; (5) referred to Juvenile Traffic Court; (6) referred, other; (7) referred to District Attorney (Adult); (8) other adult referral.

Approximately two-thirds of the males and 80% of the females in both cohorts were counselled and released by the police while the others received some type of referral. Of those in the 1942 cohort with contacts, 80% were disposed of in one way or another the same day (usually as a result of release but, of course, some by immediate referrals) and 93% within 15 days. For those in the 1949 cohort with contacts, 73% were disposed of the same day and 91% within 15 days. While a few cases in each cohort were obviously not dealt with immediately, that is, within a few weeks, only two in the 1942 cohort and 23 in the 1949 cohort had disposition dates beyond six months from time of police contact.

Since the cohort data enable us to examine the progression of careers, we are able to ascertain if referral rates (proportion of contacts referred) increase with time for

some sex, race/ethnic, and residential groups more than
for others.

As a consequence of the fact that the percent of each
cohort segment with contacts and referrals tends to fluctuate in the early years and in the later years, we have
presented percent of persons with contacts referred curves
for each cohort as 5-year moving averages in Figure 1.
The similarity of the two cohort curves up to the age 22
in the 1949 cohort is apparent. Percent with contacts
and percent referred as of any given age are the basic
curves, each curve for blacks almost always higher than
the same curve for whites. The most telling, in terms of
its suggestion of differential handling of blacks, is that
curve applying to percent of those with contacts who were
referred. At its peak in the late teens we see twice as large
a proportion of blacks as Anglos referred. Furthermore,
there is a more rapid rise in the proportion of blacks re-

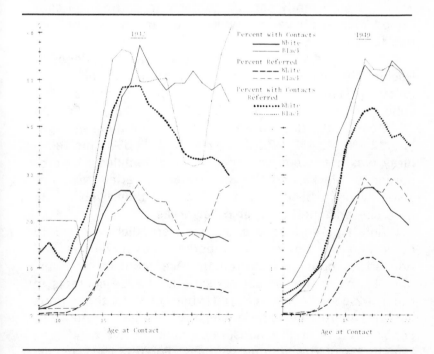

Figure 1: **PERCENT WITH POLICE CONTACTS, PERCENT REFERRED, AND
PERCENT OF PERSONS WITH CONTACTS REFERRED BY AGE:
FIVE-YEAR MOVING AVERAGES**

ferred, commencing in the early teens, than occurs for whites. And for the 1942 cohort, the gradual decline in the proportion of persons who are referred is not as apparent as is that for whites.

Smoothed curves based on an accumulation of the persons with police contacts and referrals year-by-year were also conducted. Contact curves for blacks and whites in both cohorts were essentially the same shape, but in each cohort the curves for blacks rose more rapidly and reached their peak earlier than did the curves for whites. Curves based on the accumulated proportion of those with referrals show the opposite deviation of the curve for blacks from that for whites, the proportion of the whites who were referred reaching its peak earlier and at a lower point than that for the blacks. In other words, all of the black youth who were to become involved with the police did so at an earlier age than did the whites, but the proportion who had sufficiently serious contacts to be referred continued to rise above the white peak and maintained its rise for several years.

Among those white males with continuous residence in Racine, the percent of contacts referred declined in the following sequence from Areas A through E for the 1942 cohort, 36.6%, 34.8%, 30.3%, 25.9%, and 25.3%. For the 1949 cohort the decline was similar but not quite as regular: 32.4%, 32.4%, 27.3%, 29.4%, and 25.5%. This regularity was not found for either group of females. The proportion of blacks and Chicanos referred varied less consistently on a basis of whether or not they lived in the innercity and the barrio or other areas.

When type-seriousness scores were dichotomized to determine the difference in percentage of serious and nonserious contacts referred by race/ethnicity and sex, only 14.9% of the female nonserious offense contacts in the 1942 cohort were referred while 33.3% of the serious contacts were referred. Among the females in the 1949 cohort, 16.5% of the nonserious contacts were referred but 35.2% of the serious contacts. For the 1942 males, 29.4% of the nonserious contacts were referred but 54.5% of those that were serious. In the 1949 cohort 26.9% of the nonserious contacts but 51.3% of the serious contacts were referred by the police.

To the extent that blacks had a greater proportion of serious contacts than did the whites, we would expect higher referral proportions for them. When we do control for seriousness, black females have slightly lower percentages of referrals for both serious and nonserious contacts than do white females. Black males from the 1942 cohort have higher referral proportions for both serious (65.0% versus 51.3%) and nonserious (34.7% versus 29.3%) contacts than do the whites. The disproportionately higher referral rate for even nonserious contacts at later ages for black males must be considered in light of the knowledge that the police have of prior contacts for this group. But among those from the 1949 cohort, nonserious referral proportions are the same while whites have a higher referral percentage, 53.4% versus 47.5% for the blacks. Although we investigated the possibility of a pattern of discriminatory referrals of minority groups for either more serious or less serious contacts by age periods, such was not found.

THE CHANGING LIKELIHOOD OF CONTINUING DELINQUENT AND CRIMINAL BEHAVIOR

Some individuals proceed through the various stages of what might be called developing delinquent and criminal careers, others drop out at various stages, and still others have had no contact with the police or, in some instances, have had no contacts until later stages of their lives.

Preliminary attempts to predict adult criminal careers from juvenile careers gave us mixed results. While we have constructed prediction tables for all police contacts, for traffic contacts alone, and for nontraffic reasons, only the latter is included in this report. The moderately high Tau Bs and Gammas indicate that there is some relationship between earlier and later segments of careers, but this is not the same as saying that contacts at one stage in a career are highly predictive of contacts at the following stage. To make the problem clearer, let us refer to Table

3, 1949 males, predicting police contacts at age 18 or after from contacts between the ages of 6 and 17. Kendall's Tau B is .337 and Gamma is .607, both of which suggest a moderate to high degree of association between police contact behavior in the earlier and later period for individuals. Guttman's Coefficient of Predictability (Lamba) indicates that prediction from knowledge of the predictor improves efficiency 32% over that which could be obtained by simply utilizing the modal category of the marginals at 18 or older as the category into which it would be predicted that everyone will fall.

There are two strategies that can be utilized in prediction. The first, as we have indicated, makes use of police contact status at Time 1 in predicting police contact status at Time 2. This is the Coefficient of Predictability, $E^2 - E^1/E^2$, where E^2 equals the number of errors that would be made by utilizing the modal category at Time 2 as the category into which it would be predicted everyone will fall (the nonmodal category of the predictand, $E^2 = 362$) and where E^1 equals the number of errors from knowledge of the predictor (a prediction that those with no contacts in Time 1 will have none in Time 2 and that those who have contacts in Time 1 will do so in Time 2 gives us 246). This strategy works quite well for the example cited: $362 - 246/362 = 116/362 = 32.0\%$.

The second strategy is to assume that the modal category of Time 1 is the best predictor of where everyone will be found at Time 2 on the assumption that the group will become more homogeneous as time goes by, shifting in the direction of the modal category. Whether this prediction is better than that made by the first strategy is determined by subtracting the number of errors made by predicting that everyone will be in the same modal category in Time 2 as in Time 1 from the number of errors made by knowledge of the predictor and dividing that in turn by the latter. In the example that we have just cited the result is an increase in errors: $246 - 378/246 = -132/246 = 53.7\%$. Since this strategy is of no use, why mention it? The answer is that it works well where the distribution of the marginals are quite skewed. Take the 1949 females,

Table 3: Predicting Adult Nontraffic Related Contacts from Juvenile or Juvenile and Intermediate Nontraffic Related Contacts for Persons with Continuous Racine Residence

1942 Males

		18+ No	18+ Yes	T
6-17	No	107	94	201
	Yes	50	105	155
	T	157	199	356

Tau = .209*
C of P = 8.3 -38.2
Gamma = .410

		21+ No	21+ Yes	T
6-20	No	107	60	167
	Yes	86	103	189
	T	193	163	356

Tau = .186*
C of P = 10.4 -32.2
Gamma = .362

1942 Females

		18+ No	18+ Yes	T
6-17	No	212	30	242
	Yes	22	13	35
	T	234	43	277

Tau = .227*
C of P = -20.9 17.3
Gamma = .614

		21+ No	21+ Yes	T
6-20	No	212	19	231
	Yes	30	16	46
	T	242	35	277

Tau = .297*
C of P = -40.0 28.6
Gamma = .712

1949 Males

		18+ No	18+ Yes	T
6-17	No	240	108	348
	Yes	138	254	392
	T	378	362	740

Tau = .337*
C of P = 32.0 -53.7
Gamma = .607

		21+ No	21+ Yes	T
6-20	No	240	44	284
	Yes	257	199	456
	T	497	243	740

Tau = .291*
C of P = -23.9 -65.1
Gamma = .617

1949 Females

		18+ No	18+ Yes	T
6-17	No	372	59	431
	Yes	75	51	126
	T	447	110	557

Tau = .282*
C of P = -21.8 17.9
Gamma = .622

		21+ No	21+ Yes	T
6-20	No	372	25	397
	Yes	114	46	160
	T	486	71	557

Tau = .305*
C of P = -95.8 48.9
Gamma = .714

Significance of chi-square indicated by: * = .001
0 = .01
+ = .05

for example. We note a Kendall's Tau of .282 and a Gamma of .622 but the Coefficient of Predictability reveals that use of the predictor gives 21.8% more error than simply predicting that everyone will have the same characteristics as those in the modal category of the marginals at Time 2, i.e., none of the females will have police contacts after the age of 18. Utilization of the second strategy reduces errors in prediction by 17.9%. The fact is that the second strategy worked best in every case for the females but in none of the cases for the males in Table 3.

While the prediction strategies presented in Table 3 give the impression that little in the way of prediction can be accomplished with either males or females in either cohort, other strategies must be pursued before concluding that the simple yes or no approach by age period is not at least a fruitful beginning.

Considering total contacts rather than only nontraffic contacts, one finds that 31.2% of the males from the 1942 cohort and 27.2% from the 1949 cohort had a contact in each age period. In the 1942 and the 1949 cohorts there were also 10.4% and 24.8%, respectively, who had a contact between the ages of 6 through 17 but none after the age of 21. Among the 1942 and 1949 males there were 7.1% and 18.4% who did not have contacts as adults although they had contacts between the ages of 18 and 21. But only 3.7% of the 1942 males and 12.2% of the 1949 males who had contacts in both early periods did not do so as adults. We would not expect as much progression for the males in the 1949 cohort because they had less time for exposure as adults, but again they did progress, that is, each period with contacts increased the probability of contacts during the next period.

The picture is considerably different, however, if contacts for only nontraffic offenses are considered. These are the kinds of offenses of greatest concern to society, the behaviors that seem most threatening. Here we find less continuity with about half the proportion of males having contacts in each period as they did when all contacts were considered. Also of note is the larger proportion of males who had contacts during the juvenile period but none thereafter, 14.0% for the 1942 cohort and 18.6% for the 1949 cohort. And again, almost twice the proportion as for total contacts had no police contacts during any period. Still, and this is what highlights the difficulty in prediction, 24.1% of the 1942 cohort males and 34.7% of the 1949 cohort males had contacts at either or both of the earlier periods but none after the age of 21. Females had even less continuity in their careers than did males.

The question has been raised about the kinds of police contacts experienced after the age of 21 by those who, until 21, had had no contacts. This varied from 7.6% of the males in the 1949 cohort to 19.2% of the females in the 1942 cohort. Of 528 such contacts, 303 were for traffic, 95 for suspicion, information, or investigation, 76 for disorderly conduct, 18 for nonmoving vehicle traffic violations, 8 for liquor offenses, 7 for drug offenses, 6 for theft, 3 for fraud, 3 for sex, and 9 for robbery, forgery, assault, suicide, and so on. In essence, most of these after-21 offenses for those without previous careers were for very minor offenses.

THE INTERRELATIONSHIP OF MEASURES OF DELINQUENCY AND CRIME

In addition to being asked a series of questions about how they viewed their contacts with the police, respondents filled out a self-report sheet on which they indicated the number of times that they had actually committed offenses during each of the age periods, 6 through 13, 14 through 17, 18 through 20, and 21 and older. From these were generated two similar but not identical measures to those developed from police contact data. The first, a geometric scale, with a range in scores from 0 to 31, gave 1 point to the most frequent reason for being stopped by the police, questioning, 2 points for behavior classified as incorrigibility, to 16 points for the least frequently occurring reasons for police contact, auto theft, other major thefts, and burglary. A similar scale gave from 1 to 5 points for each of these categories and multiplied the number of offenses in each category by the weight for the category.

This scale had a range in scores from 0 to 58. From the viewpoint of practical prediction, however, a measure based on police contact data would be best. Self-report data, while interesting, is not available in the real-life juvenile justice system decision-making process.

A 26 x 26 table for each total cohort and for males and females of each cohort was constructed showing the relationship of scores for each measure for each time period to the scores of each other measure for each time period. The first question is which measure (number of police contacts, type-seriousness and geometric seriousness scores for police contacts, and self-report type-seriousness and geometric seriousness scores) for the juvenile period best predict scores for the same measure in either of the later age periods, and which measure for the 18 through 20 period best predicts scores in the adult period for the same measure?

For both cohorts and both sexes within each cohort juvenile type-seriousness scores had either the highest or closer to the highest correlation with type-seriousness scores for the 18 through 20 period than did other measures with each other for these periods. It was more difficult to decide which of these sets of scores would serve as the best predictor of scores for the period 21 or older, considering cohort and sex variation. While for the 1942 cohort, the type-seriousness self-report score for the period 6 through 13 probably best predicted self-report scores for 21 or older, the number of police contacts 6 through 17 were most highly correlated for these periods for the 1949 cohort. Again, from the viewpoint of usefulness, one of the measures based on police contact would be best, and while the simple number of police contacts does not have the highest correlations for the 1942 cohort (as it does for the 1949 cohort), either number of contacts or type-seriousness could be selected as alternatives.

The best predictions of what will happen after the age of 21 were made, of course, from scores for the 18 through 20 period. While type-seriousness scores from self-report data were most consistently correlated with type-seriousness scores for the 21 or older period, practical considerations would again suggest selecting a police contact measure in developing applications.

We concluded that predicting type-seriousness measures for one age period from type-seriousness measures for an earlier period would be the most productive course for future activity. The earliest period predicted 18 through 20 for both cohorts and the 18 through 20 period predicted the 21 or older period. While number of police contacts at the adult period may just as well be predicted from number of police contacts at earlier periods, we would opt for the type-seriousness measure because persons in the juvenile and adult justice systems are more concerned about discerning who the persons will be who continue to have contacts for more serious types of crimes than in merely those who will have the greatest number of police contacts.

The second question, "Is there a possibility that seriousness scores for the 18 through 20 or 21 and older period can better be predicted by an earlier score of a different type?" may be answered in the negative. This determination further solidified our decision to concentrate on utilization of type-seriousness scores at earlier periods in predicting type-seriousness scores at later periods, these to be incorporated with other variables in development of a prediction device.

CURRENT ACTIVITIES

Matrices of all independent and dependent variables were generated for both sexes of each cohort and for each cohort as a whole. These were inspected in the process of selecting 55 representative variables and scales from the independent variables, ones that were correlated with the dependent variables but had relatively little correlation with each other. We are in the process of regressing type-seriousness scores, age 6 through 17, 18 through 20, and 21 or older on these variables for both sexes of each cohort in order to detemine which variables in combination with all others have the greatest explanatory value for each time period for each sex of each cohort.

We shall continue the analysis, entering type-seriousness scores and a variety of dispositional variables, including judicial sanctions for the subgroup that has had an opportunity to "benefit" from them. Our goal is to maximize explanation and prediction with a minimum number of variables readily accessible to persons in the juvenile and adult justice systems.

NOTES

1. The possibility of those without continuous residence in Racine differing from others (movers versus stayers) has been dealt with in Olson (1977). Olson concluded that movers and stayers were not significantly different in their careers for the period for which comparison was possible.

2. Felony against the person consisted of the following categories if charged with a felony for robbery, assault, sex offenses, narcotics and drugs, homicide, traffic-moving vehicles, escapee, and suicide. Felony against property consisted of the following categories if charged with a felony for burglary, theft, auto theft, forgery, fraud, and violent property destruction. Major misdemeanor consisted of the following categories if charged with a misdemeanor for escapee, theft, narcotics and drugs, weapons, assault, fraud, violent property destruction, burglary, and forgery. Minor misdemeanor consisted of the following categories if charged with a misdemeanor for obscene behavior, disorderly conduct, vagrancy, liquor, sex, traffic-moving vehicles, other traffic, gambling, family-parent status, and incorrigible. Juvenile condition consisted of the following categories for juveniles: vagrancy, disorderly conduct, incorrigible, and truancy. The last category consisted of those who had a police contact for suspicion, investigation, or information.

REFERENCES

OLSON, M. R. (1977) "A longitudinal analysis of official criminal careers." Ph.D. dissertation, University of Iowa. (unpublished)

WOLFGANG, M. E., R. M. FIGLIO, and T. SELLIN (1972) Delinquency in a Birth Cohort. Chicago: Univ. of Chicago Press.

Richard R. Bennett
University of Michigan

THE EFFECTS OF EDUCATION ON POLICE VALUES AND PERFORMANCE:
A Multivariate Analysis of an Explanatory Model

For the past decade there has been overt, articulate support for upgrading police services through the employment of college-educated personnel. The major justification for this position has traditionally been the hypothesized relationship between higher education and the ability to successfully accomplish the police task. This position maintains that the complexity of the police role requires personnel who (1) are able to comprehend the enormity of the task they face, and (2) have the desire and ability to successfully perform such a task. Higher education is envisioned as affording the police these necessary prerequisites.

The need for police higher education was officially recognized as early as 1931 in the conclusions and recommendations of the National Commission on Law Observance and Enforcement (Wickersham Commission). Subsequent governmental studies and commissions have echoed this necessity. The President's Commission on

AUTHOR'S NOTE: An earlier draft of this paper was presented at the annual American Society of Criminology Meetings, 1977. Partial funding for this research was provided by the Social Research Center, Washington State University. The author wishes to express his appreciation to Jack L. Kuykendall, San Jose State University, Ineke Marshall, Youngstown State University, J. Price Foster, U.S. Office of Criminal Justice Education and Training, and Eric Poole, University of Missouri for their critical comments.

Law Enforcement and the Administration of Justice (1967), the National Advisory Commission on Civil Disorders (1968), the National Commission of the Causes and Prevention of Violence (1969), and the National Advisory Commission on Criminal Justice Standards and Goals (1973) all proclaim the need for improving performance through higher education. The President's Commission on Law Enforcement and the Administration of Justice states:

> The quality of police service will not significantly improve until higher educational requirements are established for its personnel. Due to the nature of the police task and its effect on our society, there is need to elevate educational requirements to the level of a college degree from an accredited institution for all future personnel selected to perform the functions of a police agent. The demands on the police should preclude a lower requirement for persons responsible for confronting major crime and social problems [President's Commission, 1967: 126].

The National Advisory Commission (1973) attempted to implement educational standards by presenting specific time-frame recommendations. The report reads: "The standards contained in this chapter would require all police officers to have an undergraduate degree or its equivalent no later than 1982" (National Advisory Commission, 1973: 367).

In response to governmental interest in increasing police education, the university community presently has organized more than 1,000 criminal justice oriented programs or course offerings serving over 200,000 students. To maintain these programs, an estimated 80 million dollars in direct and indirect academic assistance was spent in the last year by the federal government (National Planning Association, 1967). In all, during the last half of the last decade, tremendous amounts of effort have been directed toward promoting police higher education. This effort, however, has been expanded without first investigating the actual effects of education on police performance.

Although a recent review of criminal justice educational literature revealed the existence of approximately 960 documents concerning higher education, few of these investigations included empirical verification.[1] Rather, the vast majority of these documents base their arguments on opinion and conjecture. In addition, the literature is weakened by the absence of a conceptual framework outlining the process by which education affects performance. In short, although a need has been recognized and a tentative solution implemented, little is actually known about the relationship between police performance and education.

This chapter will attempt to fill this informational void by presenting (1) a conceptual model based on the literature and designed to investigate the relationship, (2) an empirical analysis of the model to determine its explanatory power, and (3) a discussion of the implications pertaining to performance and educational attainment.

REVIEW OF CURRENT LITERATURE CONCERNING THE EFFECTS OF EDUCATION ON POLICE PERFORMANCE

A literature review was conducted to document the parameters of current, relevant knowledge concerning the effects of education. The review revealed that current (within the last eight years) criminal justice education literature can be divided into three general categories: (1) nonempirical literature, (2) empirical research reporting findings on the relationship between education, attitudes, and values, and (3) empirical research reporting findings concerning the relationship between education and performance.

Both the empirical and nonempirical literature relating attitudes or behavior to levels of education is conflicting and ambiguous.[2,3,4] In general, this literature lacks the rigor mandatory to make conclusions meaningful (Swanson, 1977). Even when the findings demonstrate a directional relationship, the resultant relationship tends to be weak. Thus, the reported collective findings do not lend themselves to the strong causal interpretation currently being articulated by governmental, academic, and practitioner spokespersons.

The lack of meaningful interpretations results not only from conflicting evidence but from the lack of a relevant explanatory framework (Strecker, 1977; Heise, 1975; Blalock, 1964, 1969; Reynolds, 1971). Instead of investigating causal process (understanding *how* and *why* an effect is generated), the majority of current works simply report the presence or absence of a relationship. In short, the state of the art of research relative to police education/ performance is disquieting and in need of considerable improvement. Only with development of improved conceptional frameworks and research can the educational community as well as governmental commissions create informed policy.

SPECIFICATION OF THE PROPOSED MODEL

As was indicated in the preceding section, police educational literature is replete with works purporting to describe and explain the relationship between education and police performance. From a perusal of this literature, a loosely defined explanatory pattern emerges. This pattern, although limited by ambiguity, will be used as a base for model construction.

Although the works of Saunders (1970), Lankes (1970), Jagiello (1971), Gross (1973), Hoover (1975), Brandstatter and Hoover (1976), Lynch (1976), and Brown (1977) were never formalized by a tight conceptional framework or empirically tested, they imply that education does not directly affect police performance.[5] Rather, they maintain that education affects attitudes and values and that these attitudes and values, in turn, affect performance. Therefore, education is hypothesized as indirectly affecting attitudes, values, and subsequently performance. An understanding of this currently nonformalized, indirect process necessitates elaboration. Relying on the preceeding and socialization literature, the relationship between education, attitudes, and performance is implicitly defined as a cumulative causal chain consisting of (1) the effect of selected biographic variables on educational attainment, (2) the effect of education on the affiliation and influence on the police workgroup, (3) the effect of this group on value systems, and finally (4) the effect of value systems on performance. A formal conceptual model, then, should include specification of these four causal stages. Each stage (except education) will be discussed individually.

Biographic Characteristics of the Police

Social position, as defined by socioeconomic status, affects human responses to the external environment (Kohn, 1969). Similarly, an individual's socioeconomic status will affect his response to education (Secord and Beckman, 1964). This response is affected in two ways. First, the value of the education increases as socioeconomic status increases from lower to middle class. Second, socioeconomic status, given the value of education, affects selection of a college major. Since criminal justice careers have not been traditionally considered prestigious, higher socioeconomic status tends to suppress student enrollment in criminal justice curriculums. Therefore, one would expect that socioeconomic status would have a positive effect on levels of education, while having a negative effect on the selection of a criminal justice major.

The effect of socioeconomic status on other variables in the model is hypothesized as being inconsequential, since police socialization tends to neutralize its effects (Niederhoffer, 1976; Chevingy, 1969; Bennett, 1976; Skolnick, 1966; Tifft, 1974).

Education and the Police Work Group

Although it has been suggested (note 3) that education directly affects police values, it would be naive to assume that values could exist independently of the effects of the work environment. Niederhoffer (1967), Chivengy

(1969), and Harris (1973) suggest that the effect of education is supressed by the overbearing effect of the work environment.

The literature on occupational socialization identified the source of this supression as selection, affiliation, and influence of the occupational reference or work group.[6] Selection of and affiliation with a reference group is determined by the combined effects of (1) individualistic and (2) situational factors. First, factors such as the group's ability (1) to satisfy individual needs (Hartley, 1960a), (2) to prescribe similar behavior norms (Hartley, 1960a), and (3) to share the individual's personal interests (Hartley, 1968) increase the individual's eventual acceptance of the group. Thus, the greater the group's ability to fulfill these needs, the more likely the individual will select the group as a reference group.

Second, the situational factors that affect selection and influence are (1) the relative isolation of the individual from other competing need-fulfilling groups (Wheeler, 1966; Harris, 1973; Cohen, 1966; Secord and Beckman, 1964), (2) dependency, both physically and mentally, on the work group (Wamsley, 1972; Wheeler, 1966), (3) the degree of rejection of civilian attitudes (Wheeler, 1966; Wamsley, 1972), and (3) the frequency and primacy of contact with the work group (Brim, 1966; Cohen, 1966). An increase in any one or combination of these factors leads to an increase in the individual's selection of the police reference group.

Since the police literature indicates that the police occupation tends to isolate, generate dependency, ensure frequent and primary contact, and reject civilian attitudes, the police reference group is seen as a viable source of support and knowledge (i.e., an increase in situational factors increases affiliation [Skolnick, 1966; Niederhoffer, 1967; Harris, 1973; Van Maanen, 1972]. However, since police reference group values are not similar to the values inculcated through a college education, college-educated individuals tend to find police reference group affiliation difficult (i.e., an increase in the individualistic variables decreases affiliation) [Rokeach, et al., 1971; Rokeach, 1973; Smith et al., 1967; Bayley and Mendelsohn, 1969]. In short, there is a conflict between the individualistic and situational factors of reference group affiliation for the college-educated individuals. Noncollege-educated individuals do not experience this difficulty. The product of this conflict is a decrease in affiliation of college-educated individuals with the police reference group.

Given the foregoing discussion, it is reasonable to assume that college-educated individuals will have less affiliation with the police reference group and, consequently, not share similar values. Although this prediction runs counter to most of the literature on police education, it is consistent with the larger body of socialization literature and a few recent police studies (for example, see Smith and Ostrom, 1974).

In addition to levels of education, it is reasonable to expect that college major or curriculum also effect an individual's eventual affiliation with the police reference group. Majoring in criminal justice should tend to diminish the normative differences between college-educated individuals and the police reference group and thus increase group selection.

Determinants of Value Similarity

Individuals learn their social occupational roles through interaction with others who already occupy those roles (Merton, 1964; Becker et al., 1961; Harris, 1973; Sterling, 1972; Van Maanen, 1972). These others (i.e., reference group) serve as the repository of occupational skills, attitudes, and value systems.[7] Transmission of value systems is determined by the degree of affiliation (Rokeach, 1973; Williams, 1969; Seigel and Seigel, 1957; Newcomb, 1958; Sherif, 1958; Hyman et al., 1968), as well as the salience of the group for the individual (Charters and Newcomb, 1958; Kelley, 1958).

Presumably, if the individual affiliates with the police reference group, he will eventually subscribe to the group's value system. This value system, then, acts as a guide for the individual's behavior and attitudes (Shibutani, 1967; Rokeach, 1973; Williams, 1969) and will affect his performance. The degree of value similarity with the group thus depends on the degree of the individual's group affiliation. The relationship between levels of reference group affiliation and value system similarity is hypothesized as being positive.

Determinants of Police Performance

Rokeach (1973) maintains that a person's values function "to provide him with a comprehensive set of standards to guide actions, justifications, judgments, and comparisons of self and others." Work-group related value systems, then, should afford a set of standards for the individual which direct, justify, and evaluate his performance (Williams, 1969).

Value systems affect behavior through two interrelated processes (Rokeach, 1973) First, value systems act as a perceptual filter. Input which is complementary to the existing system tends to be accepted more than information which is contradictory. Second, once the selected information is processed, the individual's behavioral response is limited to the range of the system's permissible behaviors. Therefore, the value system tends to control not only what the individual perceives but how the individual responds to that perception.

Since police performance is defined, evaluated, and controlled by the value system of the work group, an individual's performance rating will be determined by the degree to which his values are similar to those of the work group. Following this reasoning, it is hypothesized that as that similarity increases, individual performance ratings will also increase.

In conclusion, it is hypothesized that education indirectly affects levels of performance through (1) the effect of reference group affiliation, (2) the reference group's effect on the individual's values, and finally (3) the effect of this similarity of values on performance. The resulting multi-

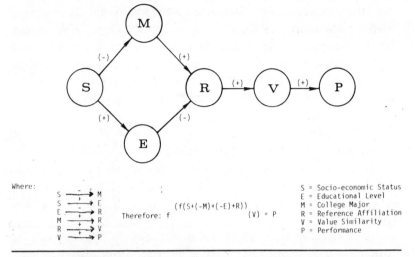

Figure 1: CONCEPTUAL MODEL FOR THE EFFECTS OF EDUCATION ON POLICE VALUE SIMILARITY AND PERFORMANCE

stage, multivariate model is pictorially summarized in Figure 1. Direction and valence of the variable relationships are also presented in Figure 1.

The preceding model was analyzed by investigating two substantive questions. The first question concerns the viability of the model in explaining the effect of education on police performance. The second question concerns the nature of the individual variable interrelationships. The predictions concerning the direction of these relationships can be found in the summary of each preceding section.

METHODS

Sample

The subjects surveyed for this study were drawn from four "purposively" sampled medium-sized, southern municipal police departments. Each of the four departments served an urban area. The departments varied in size from 329 to just over 1,000 sworn personnel. Preliminary analysis revealed that size of department was not significantly related to variance in either the independent or dependent variables. The subjects, at the time of this study, were all recruits who had completed academy training and had served three months of active "street" duty. The recruit group consisted of 103 subjects. Seven subjects were deleted from the final group due to their failure to complete the recruit training and field experience. Thus, over the nine months of the study, the study experienced a 6.4% mortality rate.

Data relevant to recruit performance were collected from each recruit's Field Training Officer (FTO: an experienced officer). The recruit was assigned an FTO based on a continuously rotating list of FTOs kept by the department. Each recruit had the same FTO for the three months of field training.

All data pertaining to this study were collected during the spring and summer 1975. This study is only one part of a larger, longitudinal study concerning occupational socialization.

Instrumentation

Since evaluation required data concerning the subject's performance as well as the subject himself, two questionnaires were devised. Both instruments were paper and pencil, self-administered questionnaires. The recruit group received a questionnaire which contained a Rokeach Value Survey, Form E,[8] four Reference Group Affiliations scales, questions pertaining to socioeconomic status (Duncan, 1961), selected college major, years of education, and other scales not relevant to the present analysis.

The subject's rank-ordering of the values was correlated with the overall median ordering of experienced officers (a random sample of those with one year or more of active duty) from the same police departments (N = 389). The resultant correlation was employed as the subject's Value Similarity score.

Reference Group Affiliation was determined by the combined, weighted proportion of police-oriented groups selected by the subject over nonpolice-oriented groups. Weights were derived from a review of Reference Group literature.[9]

The Field Training Officer's questionnaire contained seven questions tapping three general performance dimensions: attitudinal, behavioral, and relational. Scores were generated by employing a seven-point Likert summated rating procedure ("Graphic Rating Scale"). Scale weights were devised based on a review of the pertinent literature.[10] Content and construct validity of the operationalized variables was ensured through pretesting.[11]

Procedure

The recruit instrument was administered during the subject's roll call in the various departments' roll call rooms. The amount of time needed to adequately administer the questionnaire was provided by the department. The average completion time for the instrument was twenty-five minutes. Interview feedback from the subjects indicated a high level of subject sincerity in question response.

The Field Training Officer's instrument was administered at the same time as the recruit's instrument. The administration was structured so that the FTO and the recruit were not in physical proximity during the administration. The average completion time for the instrument was seven minutes. There was no respondent mortality. Postadministration interviews with the FTOs likewise revealed subject sincerity in question response. Upon completion of administration, both groups were thanked for their cooperation and were advised as to where they could secure a copy of the findings of this study.

FINDINGS

Tables 1 through 4 and Figures 2 and 3 present the findings relevant to the evaluation of the proceding research questions. The findings germane to these questions were evaluated by using a descriptive technique: path analysis. Since this study employed an ex post facto design where random assignment to treatment/control groups was impossible, significance tests or other inferential techniques are of questionable value, and thus are not

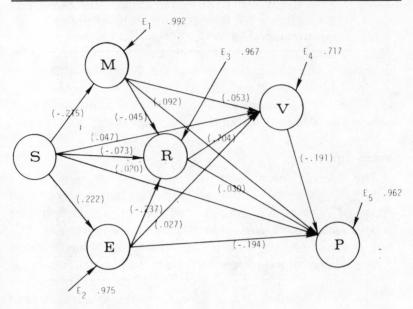

NOTE: Numbers in parenthese are standardized coefficients. Numbers not contained in parentheses refer to the disturbance terms, defined as ($R_i = \sqrt{1 - R^2}$).

Figure 2: FULLY RECURSIVE PATH MODEL FOR THE EFFECTS OF EDUCATION ON POLICE VALUE SIMILARITY AND PERFORMANCE

presented (Selvin, 1975; Blalock, 1972; Morrison and Henkle, 1969). Findings are presented by substantive question:

Question I: The proceding multivariate, multistage conceptual model adequately explains the relationship between education and performance.

Evaluation of this hypothesis necessitated investigating the simultaneous effects of the proceding variables on levels of performance. Since path analysis allows for the decomposition of empirically observed relationships into direct, indirect, and noncausal or spurious effects (Heise, 1969; Duncan, 1966, 1975; Namboodiri et al., 1975), it was considered the most appropriate analysis technique. In addition, the data met the assumptions for use of multiple regression (Blalock, 1972), the model was previously

Table 1: Path Coefficients (Standard Errors and Zero-Order Correlations for Five Determinants of Police Performance

Independent Variables	Dependent Variables				
	M	E	R	V	P
S - Socio-economic Status	-.125 (.022) [-.125]	.222 (.009) [-.222]	-.073 (.044) [-.120]	.047 (.004) [-.038]	.020 (.004) [-.031]
M - College Major	---		-.045 (2.690) [-.3352]	.053 (.249) [.068]	.092 (.244) [.142]
			[.043]		
E - Educational Level			-.237 (.514) [-.238]	.027 (.049) [-.148]	-.194 (.047) [-.199]
R - Reference Affiliation				.704 (.009) [-.694]	.030 (.013) [-.054]
V - Value Similarity					-.191 (.099) [-.136]

N = 103
a. standard error = ()
b. zero-order correlations = []

causally specified and recursive, and the disturbance terms were not assumed to be correlated (Land, 1969; Heise, 1969; Duncan, 1966; Namboodiri et al., 1975). Correlations were decomposed by using the standard "tracing" rules (Finney, 1972).

Evaluation of the first question necessitated a two-part analysis. First, the evaluation involved the comparison of predicted zero path coefficients with the observed coefficients as well as elimination of those coefficients whose values do not substantially differ from zero. Second, a reestimated model, generated from the previous analysis of the fully recursive model, is developed, presented, and decomposed.

Table 2: Comparison Between Predicted and Observed Path Coefficients

Paths	Coefficients		Decision
	Predicted	Observed	
Performance-Reference Affiliation	0	.030	delete
Performance-Major	0	.092	delete
Performance-Socio-economic Status	0	.020	delete
Performance-Education	0	-.194	retain
Value Similarity-Major	0	.053	delete
Value Similarity-Socio-economic Status	0	.047	delete
Value Similarity-Education	0	.027	delete
Reference Affiliation-Socio-economic Status	0	-.073	delete

N = 103

The fully recursive model, path coefficients, and disturbance terms are presented in Figure 2. From perusal of the information contained in this figure as well in Table 1, the zero-order correlations, standard errors, and direct effects of all independent variables on performance can be assessed.

In that the conceptual model (Figure 1) hypothesized zero path coefficients, the proposed conceptual model can be evaluated to determine if that model affords the "best fit" to the data. The criteria for comparing the predicted and the actual values are based on the degree of association desired prior to concluding that the observed value might, in fact, indicate an effect. A path coefficient of .10 or greater was selected as the criterion for retention.[12] Based on the preceding model, the following were predicted as having zero paths: P_{pr}, P_{pm}, P_{ps}, P_{pe}, P_{vm}, P_{vs}, P_{ve}, and P_{rs}. Table 3 presents the predicted and observed path coefficients. Of the eight zero predicted paths, one

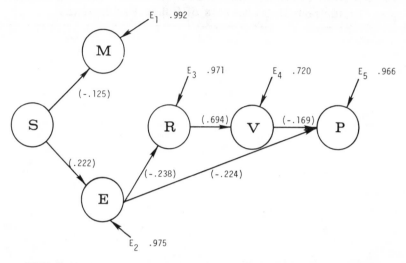

NOTE: Number in parentheses are standardized coefficients. Numbers not contained in parentheses refer to the disurbance terms, defined as: $(R_i = \sqrt{1 - R_i^2})$.

Figure 3: REESTIMATED PATH MODEL FOR THE EFFECTS OF EDUCATION ON POLICE VALUE SIMILARITY AND PERFORMANCE

was of substantial enough magnitude to be retained for the reestimated model.

Since Duncan (1966) and Heise (1969) suggest that models should be as parsimonious as possible, the model was "trimmed." Again, in accordance with the preceding discussion on the observed effects, the .10 level was selected to facilitate this process (Land, 1969; Heise, 1969). The path between reference Affiliation and Major (Prm = –.045) failed to meet the criteria and was subsequently deleted. The "new" model was subsequently reestimated. The findings relevant to this reestimation can be found in Figure 3 and Tables 3 and 4.

From examination of these tables as well as Figure 3, it is clear that the proposed model is not the "best fit" of the data. In fact, the nonpredicted and negative direct effect of Education on Performance is of greater magnitude (Ppe = –.224) than the predicted effect (.028). This finding indicates that education's effect on performance might be mediated by some other, not yet specified, causal process.

Table 3: Reestimated Path Coefficients (and Standard Error) for Five Determinants of Police Performance

Independent Variables	Dependent Variables				
	M	E	R	V	P
S – Socio-economic Status	-.125 (.002)	.122 (.009)	----	----	----
M – College Major		----	----	----	----
E – Educational Level			-.238 (.472)	----	-.224 (.043)
R – Reference Affiliation				.694 (.009)	----
V – Value Similarity					-.169 (.071)

N = 103

In addition to the models not fitting the data, the model explained so little of the variance in performance (R = .260, which accounts for only 6.5% of the variance) that the proposed conceptualization must be questioned.

In summary, evaluation of the first research question revealed that the effect of Education on Performance is slight and the proposed model is not the best fitting model. Basically, these findings contribute collaborative evidence for the empirical/performance literature which hypothesized a negligible to negative effect (see note 4). These findings, however, offer no collaborative support for those who contend that the effect of education on performance is mediated by value similarity.[13]

Question II: The observed variable interrelationships conform to prediction.

Table 4: A Summary of Reestimated Direct, Indirect, and Total Effects Plus Unanalyzed Components

Bivariate Relationship	Direct Effect	Sum of Indirect Effects	Total Effects	Sum of Unanalized Components*	Zero-order Correlations
Major - SES (P_{ms})	-.125	----	-.125	----	-.125
Education - SES (P_{es})	.222	----	.222	----	.222
Reference-Education (P_{re})	-.238	----	-.238	----	-.238
Value-Reference (P_{vr})	.694	----	.694	----	.694
Performance-Value (P_{pv})	-.169	----	-.169	.034	-.135
Performance-Education (P_{pe})	-.224	.028	-.196	-.003	-.199

N = 103
*Includes rounding error

Evaluation of this question necessitates a discussion of those observed interrelationships that conform to the model's prediction and those that did not.

The effect of the variable, socioeconomic status, conformed to prediction, in that it positively affected Educational Level (Pes = .222) while negatively affecting selection of a police college major (Pem = –.125). Furthermore, as predicted, SES did not directly affect any other variable in the model. Similarly, educational level was observed as having the predicted negative effect on Reference Affiliation (Pre = –.238) as well as not having any direct effect on Value Similarity. This finding somewhat supports the contention that education's affect on values is mediated by reference group affiliation and influence.

Finally, all but one of the predicted zero paths was, in fact, zero. Again, it must be emphasized that even though these predicted variable interrelationships were observed, their relationship is tenuous.

Although few nonpredicted variable interrelationships existed, their presence negated the utility of the model. First, and of major importance, was the nonpredicted, direct, negative relationship between Educational Level and Performance (Ppe = –.224). This nonpredicted direct relationship explained over 80% of what the entire model was attempting to explain (5.01% of the entire 6.5%). Thus the efficacy of the model is questioned. Second, the overall indirect effect was not predicted (+.028). Third, College Major had no effect on Reference Affiliation (Prm = –.045). Finally, the relationship between Value Similarity and Performance (Pps = –.169) does not conform to prediction, in that the observed relationship is negative and weak.

In summary, although most observed relationships conform to prediction, the pivotal relationships do not. Furthermore, even for those relationships which conform to prediction, the magnitude is slight. Therefore, it must be concluded that neither the overall model or its internal relationships adequately account for the present data.[14] Caution should be used in the interpretations of these findings due to sampling limitations and sample size.

CONCLUSIONS AND IMPLICATIONS

For the past decade, vast amounts of money have been spent to upgrade criminal justice personnel. These expenditures have been made without rigorous empirical evidence which would support and justify these actions. From a review of the relevant literature, it became apparent that (1) most of the literature is based on unsubstantiated personal opinion rather than empirical evidence, (2) the empirical studies report conflicting and ambiguous findings, and (3) explanatory models amenable to verification do not, for all practical purposes, exist.

To examine this situation, the literature was again consulted and a model designed to specify causality was created. The model was tested using police survey data. From analysis of the data, it became obvious that the current reliance on the "indirect effect" model lacks empirical justification. In short, the data show that educational level has a very slight and negative effect on performance, and that the proposed model is not an adequate explanatory device.

These findings indicate that governmental, academic, and practitioner spokespersons should address some persistent questions prior to unconditionally promoting postsecondary education for criminal justice personnel (Swanson, 1977). Rather than focusing on the current debate over such issues as curriculum content, administrative control, academic and professional credentials of faculty, and so on, persons interested in the development of criminal justice personnel should address two fundamental questions: (1) what is the actual, observed effect of educational attainment on performance, and (2) if education does have some effect on performance, what is the process by which this effect is realized.

The reason for the first question is self-evident. If a program or policy is ineffective and resources could be better used elsewhere, it would seem reasonable to reallocate these resources into more efficient programs. Similarly, if educational attainment does not increase performance levels of criminal justice personnel, then other means of improving police performance should be investigated and implemented.

The reason for the second question is less self-explanatory. Even if a program is found to have an overall effect, the process by which the effect is realized must be understood if realistic, informed policy is to be generated. Thus, even if educational attainment is shown to have the desired overall effect, additional questions must be asked concerning the form, intensity, and conditions under which the effect is manifested. These questions can be evaluated through the use of causal models. Answering the second question, then, permits formation of informed policy concerning education for criminal justice personnel.

It is apparent from the findings of this study that the preceding questions have not yet been adequately answered. Although there is considerable vested interest in continuing present educational policies, such political considerations should not obscure the development and evaluation of explanatory systems and, subsequently, the quest for advancement in the field of criminal justice.

NOTES

1. The source of this particular literature review was the National Criminal Justice Reference Service, Washington, D.C. Although this review should not be considered inclusive, it can be considered an adequate representation of the available literature. Other literature cited in this manuscript includes but is not limited to the literature reviewed in the NCJRS document.

2. The nonempirical literature relevant to the relationship between education, attitudes, and performance is organized along two dimensions: program content, nature, and form; and educational effect. The first dimension includes discussion of such topics as course content (Smith, 1977; Brantingham, 1972; Kuykendall and Hernandez, 1975; Lejins, 1970; Mathias, 1969; Hoover, 1975; Moynahan, 1969), the debate between the need for education versus training (Aaron, 1965; Ashburn and Ward, 1973; Brown, 1971; Cromwell, 1972; Parker, 1973; Prout, 1972; Saunders 1970; Wilson, 1974), liberal arts versus professional education (Brown, 1974; Lankes, 1970; Moynahan, 1973; Brandstatter and Hoover, 1976), academic or practioner control of curriculum, (Aaron, 1965; Sherman, 1977; Wilson, 1974), and education and professionalism (Gourley, 1972; Gambino, 1973; Germann, 1967; Gould, 1973; Lentini, 1973; Lynch, 1976).

The latter nonempirical dimensions directly addresses the issue of the effect of education on performance. Within this context, two diametrically opposed positions emerge. The first group contends that higher education has a positive effect on both police cognitions and behavior. Proponents of this position are Brown (1974, 1977), Gross (1973), Mirich and Voris (1965), Saunders (1970), Jagiello (1971), Berkley (1969), Ricks (1977), Brown (1977), Sparling (1975), and Lynch (1976). Generally they suggest that education increases the ability to perform as well as liberalizes personal and social attitudes. Although their arguments are well developed and generally well presented, they lack empirical support and thus must be considered suspect. The second position, championed by Chevigny (1969), with support from the police personality literature, maintains that the effects of education are neutralized by the overriding effects of the organization.

Police personality literature contends that the police occupation rather than any predisposing personal factor produces the police personality. It further contends that the effects of the police occupation are such that the effects of personality and the like are masked. For further elaboration see Balch (1972), Bennett and Greenstein (1975), Bennett (1976), Galliher (1971), Genz and Lester (1976), Teevan and Dolnick (1973), Tifft (1974), Westley (1970), Carlson and Sutton (1975), and Skolnick (1966).

3. Although there does exist empirical support for arguments presented in this category, the evidence is contradictory, its concepts lack uniformity, and its conclusions are ambiguous. Three general-effect categories emerge from that literature. Evidence from this literature suggests that education can have a positive, a negative, or no effect. First, Smith et al. (1967, 1970) and Roberg (1976) represent research which finds a positive correlation between levels of education, personal attitudes, and belief systems. Basically, Smith et al. and Roberg found that the attitudes of college-educated persons differed from those not so educated. The college group was less authoritarian and dogmatic. Second, there is research which suggests that education has a negative effect on attitude development. Regoli (1976) reports that education was positively correlated

with cynicism. This research supports Niederhoffer's (1967) findings. Finally, there is a sizable body of empirical research which posits a neutral or no-effect relationship. Researchers such as Weiner (1974, 1976), Miller and Fry (1976), Gukler (1972), Rokeach et al. (1971), Smith and Ostrom (1974), and, to an extent, Dalley (1975) generally conclude that the differences in attitudes are not explained by educational level.

The attitude-objects, in these studies, ranged from perceptions about police work, authoritarianism, conservatism, professionalism, and punitiveness, to perceptions about law and minority groups. In conclusion, the empirical findings concerning the relationship between educational level and attitudes are, at best, conflicting. Although some evidence exists concerning a positive correlation, the preponderance of evidence points to a weak or nonexistent relationship.

4. Similarly, conflicting evidence has been found concerning the third relational category. Researchers such as Geary (1970, 1971), Finnigan (1976), Bozza (1973), Roberg (1976), Cohen and Chaiken (1972), Baeher et al. (1968), Trojanowicz and Nicholson (1976), Christian (1976), Cascio and Real (1976), Cascio (1977), and Witte (1969) have observed a positive relationship between levels of education and quality of performance. The actual performance they evaluated ranged from crime rates, number of police injuries, arrests, traffic accidents, securing of warrants, promotions, disciplinary actions, tenure in police service, self-reported behaviors, behavior styles, and use of discretion, to generalized and/or comprehensive measures of performance.

Conversely, another group of empirical studies presents evidence which does not support the positive educational hypothesis. Smith and Ostrom (1974), Matarazzo (1964), Levy (1966), and McGreevy (1964) find that measures such as productivity, number of injuries, assaults, sick days, turnover rate, citizen evaluation of police services, frustration tolerance, and general and comprehensive performance measures either did not correlate highly or correlated negatively with police educational level.

Again, like the empirical/cognitive literature, the empirical evidence concerning the empirical/performance question is, at least, ambiguous. Most evidence supporting the positve-effect hypothesis is reported in terms of statistical significance, and very few studies employ measures of association as analytic tools. Indeed, most researchers seem content to report significance levels. Significance levels tell nothing about the strength of the relationship. One could statistically have a significant difference (given a large sample size) while substantively having a meaningless relationship.

Statistical significance should *never* be confused with substantive significance. For further discussion see: Morrison and Henkel (1969), Mueller et al. (1971), and Selvin (1958). The positive-effect studies that report both statistical significance and measures of association report that levels of education could, at best, explain only 9% (Cascio, 1977) of the variance in performance. It would appear, then, that even within the positive-effect literature the degree of support for the effect of education on performance is minimal.

5. Liberal arts education is envisioned as the most efficient means of developing an understanding of the complexities and demands of the police function (Brown, 1974; 1977; Fickanauer, 1975; Lankes, 1970; Saunders, 1970; Hoover, 1975) and attaining democratic enforcement of the criminal law (Brandstater and Hoover, 1976; Jagiello, 1971).

6. An occupational reference group is composed of standing members of the occupation. This group serves two necessary functions for a potential member.

First, reference groups act as a transmitter of the skills, knowledge, and informal organizational policy which is needed for social existence within the organization (Kelley, 1966). Second, the group affords its members those values and attitudes needed to support and justify the use of skills, knowledge, and policy (Shibutani, 1957; Merton and Rossi, 1968; Shils, 1950; Hyman and Singer, 1968). Immersion in a particular reference group, then, tends to develop skills and modify individual values by making them more similar to the group's values (Shibutani, 1962).

7. A value system is composed of both terminal values (an enduring belief that a specific end-state of existence is personally or socially preferable to an opposite or converse end-state of existence) and instrumental values (an enduring belief that a specific mode of conduct is preferable to an opposite or converse mode of conduct).

8. The Rokeach Value Survey consists of two alphabetically arranged lists of 18 values. The respondent is instructed to "rank the values in order to their importance to YOU, as guiding principles in YOUR life."

9. For conceptual determination of performance weights see: Geary, 1970, 1971; Finnigan, 1976; Bozza, 1973; Roberg, 1976; Cohen and Chaiken, 1972; Baehr et al., 1968; Witte, 1969; Cascio, 1977; Smith and Ostrom, 1974; Levy,

10. For conceptual determination of performance weights see: Geary, 1970, 1971; Finnigan, 1976; Bozza, 1973; Roberg, 1976; Cohen and Chaiken, 1972; Baehr et al., 1968; Witte, 1969; Cascio, 1977; Smith and Ostrom, 1974; Levy, 1966; McGreevy, 1964.

11. Researchers have indicated that the currently observed lack of a relationship between educational level and performance is more a function of the imperfect measures than it is a function of faulty theory (Brown, 1977; Strecher, 1977). They contend that current operational definitions of education and years of education are inadequate to tap the true dimension of education. Further, they contend that performance, to date, has not been adequately measured because of (1) lack of appropriate performance criteria, (2) lack of adequate method to measure performance, and (3) structural and organizational limitations on the administration of measurement instruments (Strecher, 1977; Riccio and Heaply, 1977).

12. An accepted criterion for selection involves strength of association. This criterion is determined by considering two elements: first, the selection level should be proportionate to the magnitude of the combined observed paths. Second, the selection level should be commensurate with levels currently accepted in the relevant literature (Mueller et al., 1970). Therefore, given the above two considerations, the .10 level of retention/deletion was selected. The .10 level is only considered the "threshold" of association.

13. Performance is evaluated by how well a subject performs a specified task. Who evaluates the task, however, is determined by a political process currently controlled by "noneducated" individuals. If Beckman (1976) is correct, then it is possible that subjects who are educated will receive a poorer rating because (1) they possess an education, (2) more subtly, their education reduces the tendency toward blind obedience, or (3) a combination of both.

14. The arguments presented in this chapter rest on the assumption that the effects of education are measurable and that the present instruments do, in fact, measure the effects. There is a sizable body of literature that contends that there are dimensions of education which defy measurement. Furthermore, even if they were measurable, their relationship with performance ratings is so tangential and convoluted that their specification would be nearly impossible. Although

the author is aware of these agruments as well as the limitations of the present operational definitions, it is contended that the currently employed measurement assumptions do not unduly distort reality and can at least be employed as an index of the concept.

REFERENCES

AARON, T. J. (1965) "Education and professionalism in American law enforcement." Police 9: 37-41.

ASBURN, F. G. and P. E. WARD, Jr. (1973) "Education and training: the moment of truth." Police Chief: 40-41.

BAEHR, M., J. FURCON, and E. FROEMEL (1968) Psychological Assessment of Patrolman Qualifications in Relation to Field Performance. Washington, DC: Government Printing Office.

BALCH, R. W. (1972) "The police personality: fact or fiction." J. of Criminal Law, Criminology, and Police Sci. 63: 106-119.

BAYLEY, D. H. and H. MENDELSOHN (1969) Minorities and the Police: Confrontation in America. New York: Free Press.

BECKER, H. S., B. GREER, E. C. HUGES, and A. L. STRAUSS (1961) Boys in White: Student Culture in Medical School. Chicago: Univ. of Chicago Press.

BECKMAN E. (1976) "Police education and training: where are we? Where are we going." J. of Criminal Justice 4: 315-322.

BENNETT, R. R. (1976) "Police value systems: an analysis of the situational model." Presented at the American Society of Criminology Meetings, Tucson, Arizona.

——— and T. GREENSTEIN (1975) "The police personality: a test of the predispositional model." J. of Police Sci. and Admin. 3: 439-445.

BERKLEY, G. E. (1969) The Democratic Policeman. Boston: Beacon Press.

BLALOCK, H. M. (1972) Social Statistics. New York: McGraw-Hill.

——— (1969) Theory Construction: From Verbal to Mathematical Formulations. Englewood Cliffs, NJ: Prentice-Hall.

——— (1964) Causal Inferences in Nonexperimental Research. New York: W. W. Norton.

BOZZA, C. M. (1973) "Motivations guiding policeman in the arrest process." J. of Police Sci. and Admin. 1: 468-476.

BRANDSTATTER, A. F. and L. T. HOOVER (1976) "Systemic criminal justice education." J. of Criminal Justice 4: 47-55.

BRANTINGHAM, P. J. (1972) "A model curriculum for interdisciplinary education in criminology." Criminology 10: 324-335.

BRIM, O. G. (1966) "Socialization through the life cycle," pp. 3-49 in O. G. Brim and S. Wheeler, Socialization After Childhood: Two Essays. New York: John Wiley.

BROWN, L. P. (1977) "Assessment of the skill and knowledge base needed in law enforcement." Presented at Criminal Justice Human Resource Needs and the Collegiate Response. Michigan State University, East Landing, Michigan.

——— (1974) "The police and higher education." Criminology 12: 114-124.

BROWN, D. C. (1971) "Education and training: perspectives of the police role." Police 16: 21-24.

CARLSON, H. and M. S. SUTTON (1975) "The effects of different police roles on attitudes and values." J. of Psychology 91: 57-64.

CASCIO, W. F. (1977) "Formal education and police officer performance." J. of Police Sci. and Admin. 5: 89-96.

——— and L. J. REAL (1976) "Educational standards for police officer personnel." Police Chief 43: 54-55.

CHARTERS, W. W. and T. NEWCOMB (1958) "Some attitudinal effects of experimentally increased salience of a membership group," pp. 276-281 in Maccoby et al. (eds.) Readings in Social Psychology. New York: Holt, Rinehart & Winston.

CHEVIGNY, P. (1969) Police Power: Police Abuses in New York City. New York: Vintage.

CHRISTIAN, K. E. (1976) "A comparison of the behavior styles of college-educated and non-college police officers." Michigan State University. (unpublished)

COHEN, A. (1966) Deviance and Control. Englewood Cliffs, NJ: Prentice-Hall.

COHEN, B. and J. M. CHAIKEN (1972) Police Background Characteristics and Performance. New York: Rand Institute.

CROMWELL, P. F., Jr. (1972) "Training-education-community understanding." Police Chief 39: 54-56.

DALLEY, A. F. (1975) "University vs. non-university graduated policeman: a study of police attitudes." J. of Police Sci. and Admin. 3: 458-468.

DUNCAN, O. D. (1975) Introduction to Structural Equation Models. New York: Academic Press.

——— (1966) "Path analysis: Sociological examples." Amer. J. of Sociology 72: 1-16.

——— (1961) "Socioeconomic index for occupations," pp. 262-263 in A. J. Reiss, Occupations and Social Status. New York: Free Press.

FENDRICH, J. F. (1967) "Perceived reference group support: racial attitudes and overt behavior." Amer. Soc. Rev. 32 (December): 960-970.

FICKENAUER, J. O. (1975) "Higher education and police discretion." J. of Police Sci. and Admin. 3: 450-457.

FINNEY, J. M. (1972) "Indirect effects in path analysis." Soc. Methods and Research 1: 175-186.

FINNIGAN, J. C. (1976) "A study of relationships between college education and police performance in Baltimore, Maryland." Police Chief: 60-62.

GALLIHER, J. F. (1971) "Explanations of police behavior: a critical review and analysis." Soc. Q. 12: 308-318.

GAMBINO, F. J. (1973) "Higher education for the police: pros and cons." Law and Order 21: 58-66.

GEARY, D. P. (1971) "Experience with college educated officers." J. of Law Enforcement Education 1: 8-11.

——— (1970) "College educated cops—three years later." Police Chief 37: 59-62.

GENZ, J. L. and D. LESTER (1976) "Authoritarianism in policemen as a function of experience." J. of Police Sci. and Admin. 4: 9-13.

GERMANN, A. C. (1967) "Education and professional law enforcement." J. of Criminal Law, Criminology, and Police Sci. 58: 603-609.

GOULD, E. W. (1973) "Does a policeman need to have a college degree to be a professional?" Law and Order 21: 68-69.

GOURLEY, G. D. (1972) "Higher education for police personnel." Law and Order 20: 34-37.

GROSS, S. (1973) "Higher education and police: is there a need for a closer look?" J. of Police Sci. and Admin. 1: 477-483.

GUKLER, I. B. (1972) "Higher education and policeman: attitudinal differences between freshman and senior police college students." J. of Criminal Law, Criminology and Police Sci. 63: 396-401.

HADLEY, R. G. and W. V. LEVY (1962) "Vocational development and reference groups." J. of Counseling Psychology 9: 110-114.

HARRIS, R. N. (1973) The Police Academy: An Inside View. New York: John Wiley.

HARTLEY, R. E. (1968) "Personal characteristics and acceptance of secondary groups as reference groups," pp. 247-256 in H. H. Hyman and E. Singer (eds.) Readings in Reference Group Theory and Research. New York: Free Press.

——— (1960a) "Personal needs and the acceptance of a new group as a reference group." J. of Social Psychology 51: 349-458.

——— (1960b) "Norm compatibility, norm preference, and the acceptance of new reference groups." J. of Social Psychology 52: 87-95.

HEISE, D. R. (1975) Causal Analysis. New York: John Wiley.

——— (1969) "Problems in path analysis and causal inference," pp. 38-73 in E. F. Borgatta (ed.) Sociological Methodology 1969. San Francisco: Jossey-Bass.

HOOVER, LARRY T. (1975) Police Educational Characteristics and Curricula. United States Department of Justice, Washington, DC: Government Printing Office.

HYMAN, H. H. and E. SINGER (1968) Readings in Reference Group Theory and Research. New York: Free Press.

HYMAN, H. H., C. R. WRIGHT and T. K. HOPKINS (1968) "Reference group and the maintenance of changes in attitudes and behavior," pp. 387-393 in H. Hyman and E. Singer, Readings in Reference Group Theory and Research. New York: Free Press.

JAGIELLO, R. (1971) "College education for the patrolman: necessity or irrelevance?" J. of Criminal Law, Criminology, and Police Sci. 62: 114-121.

KELLEY, H. A. (1968) "Salience of membership and resistance of change of group-anchored attitudes," pp. 297-311 in H. Hyman and E. Singer, Readings in Reference Group Theory and Research. New York: Free Press.

——— (1966) "Two functions of reference groups," pp. 210-214 in H. Proshansky and B. Seidenberg (eds.) Basic Studies in Social Psychology. New York: Holt, Rinehart & Winston.

KOHN, M. L. (1969) "Class and conformity: A study of values." Homewood, IL: Dorsey Press.

KUYKENDALL, J. L. and A. P. HERNANDEZ (1975) "A curriculum development model." Police Chief 42: 20-25.

LAND, K. C. (1969) "Principles of path analysis," pp. 3-37 in E. F. Borgatta (ed.) Sociological Methodology 1969. San Francisco: Jossey-Bass.

LANKES, G. A. (1970) "How should we educate the police." J. of Criminal Law, Criminology, and Police Sci. 61: 587-592.

LEJINS, P. P. (1970) Introducing a Law Enforcement Curriculum at a State University. United States Department of Justice, Washington, DC: Government Printing Office.

LENTINI, J. R. (1973) "Police professionalism: a plan for the future." Law and Order 21: 46-49.

LEVY, R. (1966) "Summary report on retrospective study of 5,000 peace officer personnel records." Police Yearbook, International Association of Chiefs of Police.

LYNCH, G. W. (1976) "The contributions of higher education to ethical behavior in law enforcement." J. of Criminal Justice 4: 285-290.

McGREEVY, T. J. (1964) "A field study of the relationship between the formal education levels of 566 police officers in St. Louis, Missouri, and their patrol performance records." Master's thesis, Michigan State University. (unpublished)

MATARAZZO, J. D. B. V. ALLEN, G. SASLOW, and A. N. WIENS (1964) "Characteristics of successful policemen and firemen applicants." J. of Applied Psychology 48 (February): 123-133.

MATHIAS, W. J. (1969) "A criminal justice curriculum for an urban society." Police Chief 36: 16-18.

MERTON, R. K. (1964) Social Theory and Social Structure. New York: Free Press.

——— and A. K. ROSSI (1968) "Contributions to the theory of reference group behavior," pp. 28-68 in H. H. Hyman and E. Singer (eds.) Readings in Reference Group Theory and Research. New York: Free Press.

MILLER, J. and L. FRY (1976) "Reexamining assumptions about education and professionalism in law enforcement." J. of Police Sci. and Admin. 4: 187-196.

MIRICH, J. J. and E. VORIS (1965) "Police science education in the United States: a national need." J. of Criminal Law, Criminology, and Police Sci. 56: 545-548.

MOHNAHAN, J. M. (1973) "Training the police officer in a liberal arts college. Police Chief 40: 58-60.

——— (1969) "A social science approach to education of law enforcement personnel." Police 14: 66-69.

MUELLER, J. H., K. F. SCHUESSLER, and H. L. COSTNER (1970) Statistical Reasoning in Sociology. Boston: Houghton Mifflin.

MORRISON, D. E. and R. E. HENKEL (1969) "Significance tests reconsidered." Amer. Soc. 2: 131-130.

NAMBOODIRI, N., K.L.F. CARTER, and H. M. BLALOCK Jr. (1975) Applied Multivariated Analysis and Experimental Designs. New York: McGraw-Hill.

National Advisory Commission on Civil Disorders (1968) Report of the National Advisory Commission on Civil Disorders. Washington, DC: Government Printing Office.

National Advisory Commission on Criminal Justice Standards and Goals (1973) Polie. Washington, DC: Government Printing Office.

National Commission on the Causes and Prevention of Violence (1969) To Establish, to Ensure Domestic Tranquility. Washington, DC: Government Printing Office.

National Planning Association (1976) A Nationwide Survey of Law Enforcement Criminal Justice Personnel Needs and Resources, Criminal Justice Education and Training, Vol V. Washington, DC: National Planning Association.

NEWCOMB,[1] T. M. (1971) "Persistence and regression of changed attitudes: long-range studies," pp. 381-389 in E. P. Hollander and R. G. Hunt (eds.) Current Perspectives in Social-Psychology. New York: Oxford Univ. Press.

——— (1958) "Attitude development as a function of reference groups: the Bennington study," pp. 265-275 in E. E. Maccoby, T. M. Newcomb, and E. L. Hartley, Readings in Social Psychology. New York: Holt, Rinehart & Winston.

NIEDERHOFFER, A. (1967) Behind the Shield: The Police in Urban Society. Garden City, NY: Anchor Books.

PARKER, W. L. (1973) "Training and education." Police Chief 40: 36-37.

President's Commission on Law Enforcement and the Administration of Justice (1967) Task Force Report: The Police. Washington, DC: Government Printing Office.

PROUT, R. S. (1972) "A methodology to developing an educational-training curriculum in law enforcement education." Police 16: 32-34.

REGOLI, ROBERT M. (1976) "The effects of college education on the maintenance of police cynicism." J. of Police Sci. and Admin. 4: 340-345.

REYNOLDS, P. D. (1971) A Primer in Theory Construction. Indianapolis: Bobbs-Merrill.

RICCIO, L. and J. HEAPLY (1977) "Apprehension productivity of police in large U.S. cities." J. of Criminal Justice 5: 271-278.

RICKS, T. (1977) "An examination of the academic response to law enforcement educational needs." Presented at Criminal Justice Human Resource Needs and the Collegiate Response, Michigan State University.

ROBERG, R. R. (1976) "An analysis of the relationship among higher education, belief systems and job performance of patrol officers in a municipal police department." University of Nebraska. (unpublished)

ROKEACH, M. (1973) Nature of Human Values. New York: Free Press.

——— M. G. MILLER and J. A. SNYDER (1971) "A value gap between the police and the policed." J. of Social Issues 27: 155-171.

SAUNDERS C. B. (1970) Upgrading the American Police: Education and Training for Better Law Enforcement. Washington, DC: Bookings Institution.

SECORD, P. F. and C. W. BACHMAN (1964) Social Psychology. New York: McGraw-Hill.

SELVIN, H. C. (1958) "A critique of tests of significance in survey research." Amer. Soc. Rev. 23: 519-527.

SHERIF, M. (1958) "Group influences upon the formation of norms and attitudes," pp. 219-232 in E. Maccoby et al., Readings in Social Psychology. New York: Holt, Rinehart & Winston.

SHERMAN, L. W. (1977) "Content and control of college curricula for the police." Presented at Criminal Justice Human Resource Needs and the Collegiate Response, Michigan State University.

SHIBUTANI, T. (1967) "Reference groups as perspectives," pp. 74-83 in E. P. Hollander and R. G. Hunt (eds.) Current Perspectives in Social Psychology. New York: Oxford Univ. Press.

——— (1962) "Reference groups and social control," pp. 128-147 in A. M. Rose (ed.) Human Behavior and Social Processes. Boston: Houghton Mifflin.

SHILS, E. A. (1950) "Primary groups in the American Army," pp. 16-39 in R. K. Merton and P. Lazarsfeld (eds.) Continuities in Social Research. New York: Free Press.

SIEGEL, A. E. and S. SIEGEL (1957) "Reference groups, membership groups and attitude change." J. of Abnormal and Social Psychology 55: 391-398.

SKOLNICK, J. H. (1966) Justice Without Trial: Law Enforcement in a Democratic Society. New York: John Wiley.

SMITH, A. B., B. LOCKE, and A. FENSTER (1970) "Authoritarianism in policeman who are college graduates and non-college police." J. of Criminal Law, Criminology, and Police Sci. 61 (June): 313-315.

SMITH, A. B., B. LOCKE, and W. F. WALKER (1967) "Authoritarianism in college and non-college oriented police." J. of Criminal Law, Criminology, and Police Sci. 58: 128-132.

SMITH, C. P. (1977) "Is relevant criminal justice education possible." Presented at Criminal Justice Human Resources Needs and the Collegiate Response, Michigan State University.

SMITH, D. C. and E. OSTROM (1974) "The effects of training and education on police attitudes and performance a preliminary analysis," pp. 45-81 in H. Jacob (ed.) The Potential for Reform of Criminal Justice. Beverly Hill, CA: Sage.

SPARLING, C. L. (1975) "The use of educational standards as selection criteria in police agencies: a review." J. of Police Sci. and Admin. 3: 332-335.

STERLING, J. W. (1972) Changes in Role Concepts of Police Officers. Washington, DC: International Association of Chiefs of Police.

STRECKER, V. (1977) "Comments on criminal justice education and manpower." Presented at Criminal Justice Human Resource Needs and the Collegiate Response, Michigan State University.

SWANSON, C. R. (1977) "An uneasy look at college education on the police organization." J. of Criminal Justice 5: 311-320.

TEEVAN, J. J. and B. DOLNICK (1973) "The values of the police: a reconsideration and interpretation." J. of Police Sci. and Admin. 1: 366-369.

TIFFT, L. L. (1974) "The 'cop personality' reconsidered." J. of Police Sci. and Admin. 2: 266-278.

TROJANOWICZ, R. C. and T. G. NICHOLSON (1976) "A comparison of behavioral styles of college graduate police officers vs. noncollege-going police officers." Police Chief 43: 56-59.

VAN MAANEN, J. (1972) "Pledging the police: a study of selected aspects of recruit socialization in a large, urban police department." Ph.D. disseration, University of California, Irvine.

WALLACE, S. E. (1966) "Reference group behavior in occupational role socialization." Soc. Q. 7 (Summer): 366-372.

WAMSLEY, G. L. (1972) "Contrasting institutions of air force socialization: happenstance or bellwether." Amer. J. of Sociology 7: 399-417.

WEINER, N. L. (1976) "The educated policeman." J. of Police Sci. and Admin. 4: 450-457.

——— (1974) "The effect of education on police attitudes." J. of Criminal Justice 2: 317-328.

WHEELER, S. (1966) "The structure of formally organized socialization settings," pp. 53-116 in O. Brim and S. Wheeler, Sociolization After Childhood: Two Essays. New York: John Wiley.

WESTLEY, W. A. (1970) Violence and the Police: A Sociological Study of Law, Custom, and Morality. Cambridge, MA: MIT Press.

WILLIAMS, R. (1969) "Individual and group values," pp. 20-37 in E. F. Borgatta (ed.) Social Psychology: Readings and Perspective. Chicago: Rand McNally.

WILSON, B. W. (1974) "Education and training: an assessment of where we are and where we are going." Police Chief 41: 23-24, 71.

WITTE, R. P. (1969) "The dumb cop." Police Chief 36: 37-38.

ABOUT THE AUTHORS

RICHARD R. BENNETT received his Ph.D. in Sociology from Washington State University. He is currently an Associate Research Scientist at the Highway Safety Research Institute, the University of Michigan. He has published in the areas of police socialization, police perception, and criminological/criminal justice theory. His current interests are in the areas of cross cultural and criminal justice model construction.

GEORGE S. BRIDGES is the administrator of small awards for the Federal Justice Research Program in the U.S. Department of Justice and a doctoral candidate at the University of Pennsylvania. His previous writing has been on issues in the measurement of crime. He is currently engaged in research examining self-reports of crime.

LARRY J. COHEN is an Assistant Professor of Political Science and Director of the Office for Law-Related Research at the University of Illinois at Chicago Circle. He is also the coeditor of an interdisciplinary journal, *Law and Policy Quarterly*. His research is concerned with legal social control policy and with disprocessing in formal and informal settings.

DEBORAH M. GALVIN is a Ph.D. candidate at the University of Pennsylvania where she is also a research associate. She has taught at American University and the University of Maryland. In addition, she has authored several papers in the areas of victimology, perception of crime by youth, and private security issues. She has worked as a consultant on numerous projects including the Private Security Advisory Council, Hallcrest Systems and PRC/PMS. She has been a recipient of a research fellowship from NIMH and a grant from the National Science Foundation.

CHARLES H. LOGAN, Associate Professor of Sociology, the University of Connecticut, has published articles on evaluation research and deterrence in the *Journal of Criminal Law, Criminology and Police Science, Law and Society Review, Social Forces,* and *Social Science Quarterly*. He is currently studying the impact of the deinstitutionalization of juvenile status offenders as well as conducting further research on deterrence.

JOAN PETERSILIA is a reseach criminologist with the Rand Corporation. Her interests center on the topics of police investigation and habitual criminals. She is the author of *Criminal Careers of Habitual Felons and The Criminal Investigation Process,* as well as numerous articles. She is currently involved in research designed to examine the characteristics of habitual criminals and the way they are treated by various criminal justice agencies.

LYLE W. SHANNON is Director of the Iowa Urban Community Research Center and Professor of Sociology in the Department of Sociology at the University of Iowa. He has been involved in longitudinal research projects in Racine, Wisconsin, since the 1950s, one a study of minority group absorption *(Minority Migrants in the Urban Community,* Sage, 1973), and the other, his current study of three birth cohorts.

GIDEON VIGDERHOUS, who received his Ph.D. in Sociology from the University of Illinois at Urbana, is a Survey Analyst at Bell Canada. The research group with which he is affiliated conducts research on public relations, corporate performance, advertising, and so on. Among his areas of interest is the application of various quantitative methods to survey and criminological research. He has published in various sociological and marketing journals.

CHARLES F. WELLFORD, received his Ph.D. in Sociology from the University of Pennsylvania and is currently Deputy Administrator of the Federal Justice Research Program in the United States Department of Justice. He serves as an Executive Counselor of the American Society of Criminology and as editorial consultant for the *Journal of Criminal Law and Criminology* and *Criminology.* Dr. Wellford has published in numerous sociological and criminological journals. His current interests include research on sentencing, deterrence, and the application of criminological theory.